FOUL FOOTBALL

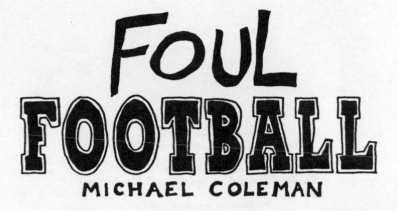

MICHAEL COLEMAN

Illustrated by
Harry Venning

Scholastic Children's Books,
Commonwealth House, 1–19 New Oxford Street,
London WC1A 1NU, UK
A division of Scholastic Ltd
London ~ New York ~ Toronto ~ Sydney ~ Auckland

Published by Scholastic Ltd 1997
Text copyright © Michael Coleman 1997
Illustrations copyright © Harry Venning 1997
Cover illustration copyright © Philip Reeve 1997

ISBN 0 590 19098 9

Typeset by TW Typesetting, Midsomer Norton, Avon
Printed by Cox & Wyman Ltd, Reading, Berks

10 9 8 7 6 5 4 3 2

The right of Michael Coleman and Harry Venning to be identified as the author
and illustrator of this work respectively has been asserted by them in accordance
with the Copyright, Designs and Patents Act, 1988.

Contents

Introduction   7

Foul Football   10

Foul Footballers   26

Foul Football Clubs   47

Foul Football Competitions   68

Foul Foreign Football   86

Foul Football Managers   97

Foul Referees   115

Foul Fans   126

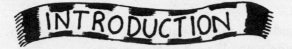

Are you a foul footballer? Of course you aren't, otherwise you'd be kicking this book instead of reading it! No, I bet you're somebody who simply enjoys playing the best, the most exciting, game in the world.

So, what do you like best about playing football?

- scoring loads of great goals?
- getting in plenty of terrific tackles?
- scaring the other team with some dreamy dribbling (not the messy sort!)?
- walloping fearsome free-kicks?
- being stamped on, beaten up and generally hacked to bits?

Well, unless you enjoy playing against really foul teams (a team of teachers, for instance) then you probably didn't pick the last option!

If you'd been playing football when the game first began, though, that would definitely have been your choice – because that was what football was all about. There were very few rules. Stamping, hacking, and generally beating up the players on the other side was all part of the game.

It's a wonder the game didn't end up being called foot-brawl instead of football!

What's more, if you didn't end up in hospital you could end up in jail. Football was often banned because it was so rough. It's said that King Richard II stopped his soldiers playing a game of football – because he was afraid they'd all be too crocked to fight the French army!

Nowadays things are a bit different. Football is played the world over, by boys and girls, men and women. It's a great game, full of skill. There are strict rules, and the best footballers are those that everybody else is frightened of playing against because they're so good, not because they're big and mean and ugly (unless they play for a team of teachers...).

Of course, this doesn't mean that you won't meet some pretty foul footballers in this book. You certainly will!

You'll meet:
- foul footballers and fair footballers
- fair teams and foul teams ... and their foul managers!

You'll read about:
- some fair trophy-winners...
- and some foul flops!

And you'll even discover some frightening facts about:
- foul referees!
- and foul fans!

So start reading ... but if you're reading in class, watch out for your teacher. You don't want to get fouled!

There is a legend that English football began in the 8th century. The Saxons and the Vikings had just had a big battle (the first international match!) which the Saxons had won. The beaten Viking squad had gone away empty-handed. Worse, at least one of them had ended up empty-shouldered as well – a Saxon had cut off his head as a souvenir!

But what can you do with a spare head?

At which point they all looked at each other and shouted: "Yeh! That's what we'll do with it!"

And so they did – they used the Viking's head as a football!

Putting the boot in

However the game really started, "foot-balle" (as it was known) was certainly played in medieval times. A real foul game it was, too! You wouldn't have persuaded King Edward II to give out the medals at the Cup Final – early in the 14th century he issued a proclamation banning the game:

Forasmuch as there is a great noise in the city caused by hustling over large balls, from which many evils may arise, we command and forbid on behalf of the King, on pain of imprisonment, such game to be used in the city in future.

But over two hundred years later the game was still being played – and, if anything, it had become even fouler! Philip Stubbes was a Puritan who wrote, in 1583, about the nasty goings-on that he thought needed to be stamped out:

As concerning footballe playing, I protest unto you that it may be called a friendlie kind of fight....

In 1829 a big game took place in Derbyshire. The match report talked of many players:

"...falling, bleeding beneath the feet of the surrounding mob."

Sounds more like a game in your school playground, doesn't it?

But, in spite of all this, the game survived. Even though Kings may not have liked it, the peasants did. They'd play it on Sundays – presumably because, after being down-trodden by their masters all week, it gave them a chance to do some down-treading of their own.

A game called "hurling at goales" was popular in Cornwall in the 16th and 17th centuries and, in the 17th and 18th centuries a game called 'kicking camp' was played in East Anglia (bad news if your name was Camp!).

These games were between neighbouring villages. They would often play each other on a special day, just once a year – probably because it took them that long to recover!

Did you know?

A favourite day for playing foot-balle was Shrove Tuesday, the day we still call "pancake day". Maybe this was because a lot of the players ended the game as flat as one!

Perhaps you'd like to try setting up a school foot-balle match of your own. Here's how to do it:

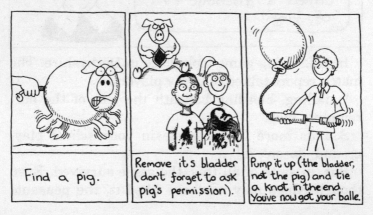

Find a pig.

Remove its bladder (don't forget to ask pig's permission).

Pump it up (the bladder, not the pig) and tie a knot in the end. You've now got your balle.

Pick your school team. This is easy. Everybody can play! (Forget 11-a-side. For a good game of foot-balle you want at least 150-a-side!!)

Send out a challenge to the school down the road.

Find a pitch to play on. The road between your school and theirs is perfect.

At the start of the game your team goes to the end of the road and their team to the other.

Somebody throws the balle into the middle of the road - and then both teams.....

CHARGE!

The aim of the game is to score goals, of course. Your team is aiming to get the ball into the other school's goal which is at their end of the road. How you get it there doesn't matter. You can kick it, pick it up and throw it, pick up the person who's got the ball and throw them... The referee won't stop you, for the simple reason that there isn't one – who needs a ref when there aren't any rules?

Foul football rules

Rules arrived in the middle of the 19th century. By then, football was a popular game at public schools, like Eton and Harrow. What they'd done, though, was to take the foul village punch-up kind of football and turn it into a sport with some rules.

The problem, though, was that each school devised their own rules. This made life pretty tricky when they wanted to play against each other. (If you're not sure why, try to imagine playing a school football match against a team who think you're playing rugby!) So, in 1863, after a couple of false starts, the first set of rules was adopted.

They were known as the 'Cambridge Rules' because they were first tried out in a game at Cambridge University.

Cambridge Rules, O.K.?

So, try this quiz. Which of these were in the Cambridge Rules?

1. The pitch could be up to 200 yards (183m) long x 100 yards (91m) wide – YES/NO
2. The goalposts had to be 8 yards (7.3m) apart, but could be as high as you liked – YES/NO
3. To score a goal the ball had to be kicked between the posts – YES/NO
4. Teams changed ends every time a goal was scored – YES/NO
5. When the ball went off at the side of the pitch it had to be thrown in again. No player was allowed to touch the ball until it hit the ground – YES/NO
6. If one of the other team kicked the ball behind your goal then your team got a goal-kick, but if

one of your players touched it last the other team got a free kick! – YES/NO

7. Any player could catch the ball, but not run with it – YES/NO

8. Picking the ball up, or passing it with the hands, was forbidden – YES/NO

9. The ball could only be passed backwards, not forwards – YES/NO

10. You couldn't trip, hack, hold or push ... and you weren't allowed to wear boots with nails sticking out of the bottom – YES/NO

Answers: YES! They were ALL in the Cambridge Rules!

1. Nowadays the pitch can't be bigger than 130 yards x 100 yards (91m).

2. There was no limit to the height of the goal! Great for hoofers!

3. Crossbars weren't invented until much later.

4. Pretty boring if the score was 50-0!

5. And throw-ins had to be taken one-handed!

6. The penalty was actually called a free kick and had to be taken in line with wherever the ball went out.

7. After catching the ball, you could make a mark on the pitch with your heel; you were then awarded a free-kick.

8. You could only pass the ball by kicking it.

9. If you were in front of the ball you were 'offside'. You weren't allowed to touch the ball or tackle anybody.

10. You weren't allowed iron plates on the bottom your boots either!

15

As you can see, football played by the Cambridge Rules was pretty different to the game we know now. It was much more like rugby. In fact rules 2, 3, 5 and 9 are still in the game of rugby as it's played today.

Football rulers – The Football Association

The Football Association (or F.A. as it is usually known) was formed in 1863 by a number of football clubs in the London area. The idea was that the F.A. would publish a set of agreed football rules, and these would be the rules used when any of the F.A.s member clubs played each other.

Starting with the Cambridge Rules, the clubs had a meeting ... and another meeting ... and another...

This was the moment when Rugby and Association Football parted company. Blackheath went off to help begin the Rugby Union, whilst the other F.A. members set about developing the game we know today.

Fair women and foul officials

Once the game started to get a bit organized, women
decided they'd play it too.

Unfortunately, that's when they ran into some
foul officials!

The British Ladies Football Club was formed in
the 1890s by the perfectly-named Nettie Honeyball.

A crowd of 10,000 turned out to
watch their first game! The
trouble was, some of the crowd
were officials of the F.A. who
described the game as "a farce".
They thought football was a
man's game, and that the
whole idea of women playing
football was daft.

In 1902, they banned all their member teams from
playing against women's teams and, in 1921, even
went as far as to ban them from playing games on
the grounds of league teams.

They were probably jealous. A very well-known
team, formed in 1894, was called Dick Kerr's
Ladies. They toured the country (they even went to
America) playing games to raise money for charity.

17

In 1917, in the middle of the First World War, they'd even played at Goodison Park, home of Everton, to raise money for a military hospital.

How big was the crowd for that game?

a) 15,000

b) 20,000

c) 25,000

Answer: Sorry, you've been fouled – it was none of them. The crowd was actually 50,000! No wonder the F.A. didn't like them. In 1915, before the war had started, the real Everton team had only averaged crowds of 18,500!

It wasn't until over 50 years later, in 1969, that the Football Association finally recognized that girls and women had a right to play football too. Now there's a Women's F.A., hundreds of women's football clubs, and a full programme of national and international competitions.

But it's not all good news. The F.A. still won't let women's teams play against men's teams. They won't even let girls play in the same team as boys! Maybe they're worried that the girls will be better? Whatever the reason, they'll have to change their mind one day. In the meantime, girls, keep on playing the game. And no fouling!

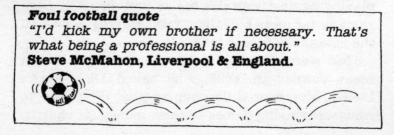

Foul football quote
"I'd kick my own brother if necessary. That's what being a professional is all about."
Steve McMahon, Liverpool & England.

No fouls! The laws of football timeline

The rules, or laws, of football have often changed – usually to stop some foul footballer who'd thought of a sneaky way of getting round them! Here's how...

1865 To stop games ending up 75-all, the goals were reduced from as-high-as-you-liked to just 8ft (2.4m). This was done by simply stretching a tape between the posts.

1871 The size and weight of the ball was fixed. Its circumference had to be somewhere between 8.5cm and 71cm, and weigh between 397gm and 454gm. So, no Viking heads!

1871 Goalkeepers were mentioned in the rules for the first time. Until this date everybody was allowed to catch the ball – so everybody was a goalkeeper! Now, only a team's goalkeeper could catch the ball. Who was the goalkeeper? The player nearest the goal – so everybody was still a goalkeeper!

1872 Instead of giving away a free kick when you put the ball behind your goal, corner kicks were invented instead.

1875 The trouble with a tape across the goal was that, when the ball hit the tape, nobody knew if a goal had been scored or not. To get round this a solid crossbar was introduced.

1882 Throw-ins now had to be taken two-handed; up until now they'd been taken one-handed.

1890 Goal nets were introduced to help referees decide if the ball had gone between the posts.

1890 – 1892 Perilous penalties!

Of all the rule changes, those that have kicked up most fuss have been to do with penalty kicks.

This is what happened in the 1890 F.A. Cup quarter final between Notts County and Stoke...

20

Sorry, penalties weren't invented at that time. All poor old Stoke got was a free-kick which the Notts County goalkeeper easily smothered. (The rule making him stand ten yards away didn't exist either, remember!)

After this, in 1891, penalties – and penalty areas – were invented. Even then, some F.A. members objected. They thought a penalty law suggested that some of their players were ungentlemanly ... which they were, of course!

Then, only a year later, this happened in the match between Aston Villa and Stoke...

Villa are desperately hanging on to their 1-0 lead.... It's Stoke on the attack. It looks dangerous... It is dangerous! Foul! Stoke have got a penalty with just two minutes to go. It's their chance to equalise – so long as they can find the ball...

As the referee gave the penalty, Aston Villa's goalkeeper promptly picked the ball up and booted it out of the ground. By the time they'd got it back, time was up and Villa were the winners. After this, the rule was changed to allow extra time to be added on so that a penalty could be taken. As if that wasn't enough, another change came in 1892. Why? Because this was how you could take penalties at that time...

Bloggs runs in to take the penalty. Here he comes... Hello, what's he doing? He's dribbling the ball forward!.....He's taking it closer to the goal! Wallop!! Yep, he's scored.....

Yes, it didn't have to be a penalty kick – it could be a penalty dribble! This made scoring penalties so easy that the rule was changed once again, this time to say that the penalty taker could only touch the ball once.

1912 Until now, goalkeepers had been allowed to handle the ball anywhere in their own half! This meant they could catch the ball near the halfway line and then try to belt it back into the other team's goal! After both goalkeepers had done this in one match the rule was changed to stop them handling the ball outside their own penalty area.

Stay in the Penalty Box! Blimey! Next they'll be saying I can only take four steps!

Actually, lads, you're supposed to stand the other side.

1913 Getting a free-kick wasn't a lot of use sometimes because the laws allowed the other team to stand just 6 yards (about 5 metres) from the ball! Now a rule was brought in to make them stand at least ten yards (over 9m) away.

1914 The ten-yard rule was extended to cover corner kicks as well.

1924 Goals could be scored from corners.

1925 Somebody cut a corner! Everton beat Tottenham 1-0 after their winger Sam Chedgozy took a corner by dribbling the ball forward and then whacking it into the net! The rule was changed to say that the kicker could only touch the ball once.

1925 The 'orrible off-side rule was changed as well. This said that, when a player has passed the ball, at least *three* of the other team had to be between him and their goal. If they weren't then the player was offside and a free-kick was given. Defenders loved it! They'd become so good at "trapping" forwards offside that some matches were all free-kicks and no decent kicks. In 1925 the

rule was changed to *two* defenders. And now the forwards loved it! On the first day under the new rule, Aston Villa scored 10 against Burnley!

1929 When facing a penalty, goalkeepers weren't allowed to move before the ball was kicked.

1937 Defenders weren't allowed to tap the ball into their goalie's hands from a goal kick.

1981 The International F.A., F.I.F.A., accused footballers of becoming plonkers when they said that there was too much kissing going on. No law was brought in to stop it, though.

1992 Goalkeepers are not allowed to handle backpasses.

Foul football question

When were kick-ins used instead of throw-ins?

Answer:

1993! An international trial was carried out. In England, the clubs in the semi-professional I.C.I.S. League had to play by this rule.

So, that's how the rules of the game have developed since 1863. Could the founders of the F.A. have imagined that football would grow into the most popular game in the world?

Perhaps they could. Even then competitions had started, and new teams were springing up everywhere. Before very long, footballers were starting to become famous – some of them foul and famous!

So come on, lace up your boots. Check your studs. Ready?

Right, off we go. Up the player's tunnel, and on to the pitch. Let's see who we meet!

What makes a footballer?

Thousands of footballers have thrilled crowds since the game began. So, if you're going to become a footballer, what do you need to worry about?

Age anguish

Young or old, you can be a footballer. Scottish goal-keeper Ronnie Simpson (Queens Park, 1945) played his first game at the age of 14 years, 304 days! Alan Shearer (Southampton, 1988) became the youngest player to score a 1st Division hat-trick when he banged in three goals against Arsenal at the tender age of 17 years 240 days. And as for being too old, the legendary Stanley Matthews (Stoke, 1965) played his last game at the age of 50 years, 5 days!

Foul football question

On the last day of the 1950/51 season, Alec Herd watched his 17 year-old son David play for Stock-  port. At the same time, David watched his 39 year-old dad Alec play against Hartlepool. How did they manage it?

Answer:

Father and son were both playing for Stockport v Hartlepool!

How tall?

It doesn't matter how tall you are, either!

You can be very tall, like goalkeeper Albert Iremonger (Notts Co, 1900s) who was 1.98m, 5cm taller than the current England goalkeeper David Seaman (Arsenal). What's more, if anything annoyed Iremonger during a game he'd just sit on the ball in the middle of the field and, until things were put right, nobody could get him off it! In other words, Iremonger didn't bawl and shout, he

balled and sat! On the other foot, you can be pretty short, like Alex James (Arsenal, 1930s). When he played against Walsall in the F.A. Cup, there was a hole in the changing room wall, which the Walsall players peeped through. They saw that James had to stand on the bench to reach his changing room peg!

How heavy?

It doesn't even matter how heavy you are.

The enormous goalie "Fatty" Foulke (Sheffield Utd, 1900s) weighed nearly 140kg. Next to him, Peter Schmeichel at 85kg would have looked like Schmeichel the schrimp! Foulke was an amazing character. His goal kicks sailed to the other penalty area, and he could punch the ball to the halfway line. And how do you think he dealt with foul forwards who annoyed him? He picked them up and dangled them by their ankles!

At the other end of the scales, the famous Scottish footballer, Patsy Gallagher (Celtic, 1910-20s) weighed in at a mere 45kg – not much more than a cow-patsy! Compare him to Robbie Fowler at 73kg and Ryan Giggs at 68kg.

Foul football question

Patsy Gallagher once scored a remarkable goal for Celtic. He was lying on the goal-line, facing the wrong way, and with the ball trapped between his feet. So, how did he score?

Answer:

Still holding the ball between his feet, he did a back-somersault and landed in the goal!

So, what is important if you want to become a footballer? That depends on which position you want to play. Here are some foul examples to help you along!

Gruesome goalkeepers

As goalie you're the last line of defence. Your job is to stop the ball going between the posts (does that make you a postman as well as a footballer?). You can pick the ball up, but only in your penalty area.

So, you need…

- A sticky pair of hands – but not *too* sticky, like those of Gary Sprake (Leeds, 1970s). In a game against Liverpool the ball stuck to his fingers as he went to throw it out – and he ended up throwing it into his own net instead.

- Not to mind getting dirty – unlike the Spanish international goalkeeper, Zamora. He played in the 1930s, and hated dirt and mud so much that he'd occasionally keep a broom with him and tidy up the goalmouth! Perhaps he thought he was playing sweeper instead?

- Watch the game at all times – unlike Joachim Isadore. Playing for a Brazilian team called the Corinthians against Rio Preto, he let in the fastest goal in history – after just one second! Isadore had been saying some prayers and didn't realize the game had started.

Deadly defenders and marauding midfielders

Your job is to stop the other team's attacks and, if you can, join in with your own team's attacks. It's also great if you can score a few goals. But that means that you need...

- A good sense of direction – unlike Sammy Wynne (Man Utd, 1923), who seemed to get pretty confused when his team drew 2-2 against Oldham. Sammy scored all the goals – a penalty and a free-kick at the right end, and two own-goals at the wrong end!

- Good hearing – in particular, to know what the referee's whistle sounds like. Left-back Dennis Evans (Arsenal, 1955) heard a whistle and thought it was the ref blowing for the end of their match against Blackpool. So what did he do? Boot the ball into his own goal, only to discover that it counted. He'd scored an own goal! The whistle he'd heard had been blown by somebody in the crowd. Good job Arsenal were winning 4-0 at the time!

Amazing attackers

If you're an attacker, your job is simple. You've got to bang in the goals. That means some talents are very useful to you...

● A big head – like Peter Aldis (Aston Villa, 1952) against Sunderland, when he headed a goal from the record distance of 32 metres – the only goal he scored in his career!

● Be able to score in your sleep – like Nat Lofthouse (Bolton, 1950s). Playing for England against Austria, he collided with their 'keeper, but still managed to kick the ball. He was unconscious when it went into the net!

● Ball control – like Robert Vidal (Oxford University, 1873) whose nickname was 'The Prince of Dribblers'. In those days, the rule was that the team that scored also kicked off afterwards. On one occasion this rule allowed Vidal to score three goals in a match without the other team touching the ball!

Did you know?

In the 1939 F.A. Cup Final, Portsmouth played hot favourites Wolverhampton Wanderers. They were so famous that the Portsmouth team asked for their autographs!

Finding they couldn't actually read many of them, the Portsmouth players decided that if the Wolves players couldn't write properly then they had to be a bunch of bozos.

Portsmouth went out and whacked them 4-1!

The Cheers and Boos Game

THIS WAY →

So you want to be a footballer. Try it by playing this game. The idea is to get more cheers than boos from the crowd.

KICK-OFF

FANTASTIC START TO YOUR CAREER

1 At the age of fourteen Eamonn Collins became the youngest league player when he came on as sub for Blackpool.

I would have come on earlier but I had to finish my homework first.

SCORE THREE CHEERS !

2

HALF-TIME
GO ON TO NEXT PAGE

10 GET IN THE ACTION STRAIGHT AWAY

On 25 February 1984 Colin Harris scored his 1st goal with his 1st touch in the 1st minute he was on the field in his first game for Dundee!

ZOOM

SCORE 0 CHEERS

You were too quick for anyone to see it!

9

COME OUT OF THE RESERVES AND BANG IN 10 GOALS!

8

Huh! I'd have scored at least eleven

Joe Payne was a reserve wing-half when he was picked as make-shift centre forward for Luton's game against Bristol Rovers on 13 April 1936, scoring 10 goals in their 12-nil win.

SCORE **10** CHEERS (AND 1 BOO FROM THE PLAYER REPLACED)

3

"Sorry, young Keegan, you've no chance."

FOOTBALLERS HEIGHT

TERRIBLE START TO YOUR CAREER Billy Wright, Alan Ball and Kevin Keegan – all to play for England one day – were turned down by clubs because they were too small.

SCORE 1 BOO HOO and miss turns until you're taller.

4

STRUGGLING TO GAIN RECOGNITION Liverpool and England goalkeeper Ray Clemence was a deck-chair assistant before turning professional **SIT OUT THE NEXT ROUND**

5

7 **YOU MAKE THE WRONG SORT OF HISTORY** Keith Peacock of Charlton made history on 21st August 1965. He was the first player taken off under the new substitution rule. **SCORE 1 CHEER** (from the opposing fans) and lose a turn).

FAIL TO MAKE THE GRADE AND GO TO PLAY IN ITALY Pope John Paul II was once goalkeeper for the Polish amateur team Wostlya

SCORE 1 BOO HOO AND LEAVE THE GAME. **CONSOLATION PRIZE:** millions of cheers for ever after.

6

11

THIS WAY →

SECOND HALF

FULL TIME!

"That's the most intelligent thing I've ever heard him say."

BURP!

NO STOMACH FOR THE GAME

In 1993 Paul Gascoigne was criticised for burping into a TV interviewer's microphone. **SCORE 2 BOOS** — AND MISS A TURN TO LEARN SOME MANNERS!

12

21 SUFFER FROM TOO MUCH FAME, LEAVE AND REJOIN THE GAME MANY TIMES AND FINALLY START DRINKING TOO MUCH.

George Best, idolised at Man United, left the game at the height of his fame. He tried comebacks with Fulham and Hibs. Finally admitting to drink problems he said:

"I'd go to Alcoholics Anonymous but I'd have trouble staying anonymous"

SCORE 1000S OF CHEERS – BUT YOU STILL LOSE THE GAME. YOUR BOOZE COUNT IS TOO HIGH!

SAINT, SINNER & SAINT

Between 1993 and 1996 Eric Cantona wins 3 championship medals but is banned in 1995 for Karate kicking a spectator. SCORE 1 BOO, 3 CHEERS, HAVE ANOTHER GO (BUT NOT AT A FAN!)

20

19

HIT BY MISSILE (BUT SAY WITTY THING)

Playing for Newcastle in 1982 Kevin Keegan was hit by a ball bearing thrown from the crowd. "I never saw it coming" he said "otherwise I might have scored with it!"

BONK!

SCORE 3 CHEERS AND BECOME MANAGER TEN YEARS LATER

1

SENT OFF FOR THE **1ST** TIME

"I hope you're not going to make a habit of this, Shilton."

England goalkeeper Peter Shilton was sent off for the first time when playing his 971st game.

SCORE 970 CHEERS AND 1 BOO

13

14

SENT OFF, MURDERED AND BANNED **15**

"The good news is that you can appeal against the ban next season"

In 1995 Luigi Coluccio, a Calabrian league player in Italy, was sent off. A week later he was shot dead. Even so, he was still banned, because it could have influenced the end of season fair play awards. **SCORE 3 BOOS AND LEAVE THE GAME FOREVER!**

LUIGI COLUCCIO

DROPPED! Harold Bell played 459 consecutive league and cup games for Tranmere Rovers between 1946 and 1955 before he was dropped! **SCORE 1 BOO AND 3 CHEERS, MISS A GO, BUT COLLECT A LONG SERVICE AWARD**

MATCH PROG.

"Bell isn't playing! I hope the manager hasn't dropped a clanger!"

17

16

Foul fantasy football team

Maybe you'll end up being a star player just because you've got a good name. Here's a whole team full of the foulest names in foul football history!

Ron BATTY
Newcastle (1945-58)

Eddie BOOT
Huddersfield (1937-52)

Terry BUTCHER
Ipswich (1976-86)

Jesse CARVER
Blackburn (1925-35)

Walter CROOK
Blackburn (1932-47)

Bill DODGIN
Arsenal (1952-61)

Barry FRY
Man. United (1962-69)

Leslie GORE
Fulham (1933-36)

John HACKING
Oldham (1926-34)

Peter MADDEN
Rotherham (1955-66)

Joseph MALLETT
Southampton (1947-53)

and to make up for them...

MANAGER:
Ian ST. JOHN
Portsmouth (1974-77)

Foul injuries

If you're a footballer, there's always the chance of getting injured. If you're a foul footballer there's an even better chance of course, because somebody will probably want to foul you back! So, don't be surprised if your mum's really worried.

One mum who did get worried was that of the Hon. A.F. Kinnaird. Kinnaird played in the 1880s for both the Wanderers and the Old Etonians. He appeared in nine F.A. Cup Finals and won five winner's medals, but his biggest claim to fame was his fearsome "hacking". It's said that another player, Capt Marindin, called on Kinnaird's mum one day.

MUM: He's playing that nasty football game again. I'm frightened that one day he'll come back with a broken leg.

MARINDIN: Don't worry, Mrs Kinnaird. It won't be his own!

Foul football question

Playing for Coventry in 1975, David Cross was kicked in the head by the Leeds defender, Norman Hunter. What did Hunter shout?

a) You're a nutter, Crossie!

b) Good job I hit you in the head, Crossie, or I might have hurt you!

c) You're supposed to head the ball, Crossie, not my boot!

Answer:

b) – No wonder the Leeds player was known as Norman "Bites yer legs" Hunter!

Sadly, it's not unknown for players to actually die during the game – a pretty foul way to end your career.

Goalkeepers seem to be in danger the most, usually when they rush out and dive at somebody's feet. John Thomson (Celtic, 1931) did this in a match against Rangers and died from a fractured skull. Maybe goalies should wear safety helmets like cricketers do nowadays?

Bob Benson (Arsenal, 1913) made a tragic decision, too. He'd been retired for a year after a playing career with Sheffield Utd, when he was persuaded to make a comeback with Arsenal. In the middle of his first game, against Reading, he felt ill and went off. He died in the changing room.

Thankfully, not all injuries are as bad as these. Most only result in broken bones and twisted bits! So, if you're going to be a foul footballer it's a good idea to know something about anatomy. That way you'll be able to tell the doctor which bone you've broken or bit you've twisted!

Battered bones

Try this quiz about players who've broken bones. It's a real cracker!

a) Goalkeeper Jim Blyth (Birmingham, 1982) played for over an hour in a match against Sunderland with a broken what?

b) What did Gerry Byrne (Liverpool, 1965) break after 5 minutes of the F.A. Cup Final against Leeds?

c) Dave Mackay (Tottenham, 1964) broke this when playing for Tottenham Hotspur, spent nine months recovering, then broke it again in his comeback match!

d) What did Bert Trautmann (Man City, 1956) break 15 mins from the end of the F.A. Cup Final against Birmingham?

e) During his career, Dennis Smith (Stoke, 1970s) broke how many bones?

Answers:

a) Right arm – broken in 3 places!

b) Collar bone. He played out the remaining 85mins … and then 30 mins of extra time!

c) Left leg. It didn't stop him though. Mackay went on to win the F.A. Cup with Spurs and the Second Division championship with Derby County.

d) Neck! He played on, though – and went up to get his medal!

e) Twelve! That's not counting the six little cracks to various fingers and toes!

Finally, there was the case of 19 year-old Frank Swift (Manchester City, 1934) who collapsed at the end of the F.A. Cup Final against Portsmouth. He hadn't broken anything, though. He'd simply fainted!

When I said fetch the magic sponge that's not what I meant.

Foul football boots

Surprisingly enough, footballers don't wear much in the way of protection. The only hard bits (apart from their heads) are the boots on their feet and the shinpads on their legs.

Shinpads, or shinguards as they were called, were originally worn *outside* your socks! They were made out of strips of cane, encased in leather. They looked a bit like a small pair of cricket pads.

Shinguards worn inside the socks were invented in 1874. A man named Sam Widdowson invented them for himself. Why? Have a look at what football boots were like in those days...

Pretty foul, eh? And until the 1960s that's the sort you'd have had to wear! That's when the lightweight boots we see nowadays, with either screw-in studs or moulded soles, were invented. They make ball-control much easier – and tricky-winger-control much harder!

Freak fouls: crazy injuries

Not all injuries are the result of being kicked, though. Some footballers have been injured in very curious ways. Try this foul quiz...

1. Chris Brodie (Brentford, 1970) was playing against Colchester when he was injured in a tackle with:

    a) the referee

    b) a small dog

    c) a spectator

... and don't complain or I'll book you for arguing with the ref!

2. England goalkeeper Chris Woods (1990) was trying to undo his track suit trousers when:

    a) he stabbed himself with a penknife

    b) the elastic snapped and broke his finger

    c) a button flew up and hit him in the eye

CRUNCH!

3. Steve Morrow (Arsenal, 1993) scored the winner for his team in the League Cup Final and then had his arm broken by:

    a) running into a goalpost

    b) being congratulated

    c) doing a somersault

4. Goalkeeper Dave Beasant (Southampton, 1993) injured his foot when:
   a) his wife ran over it in the car
   b) another player April Fooled him with a concrete football
   c) he dropped something on his own toe.

Stanley Matthews – the wizard of the dribble

Stanley Matthews played top-class football for an amazing 33 years. He was born in 1915 and played his first game for his home-town club, Stoke City, when he was 17.

Matthews was a right-winger. This was his favourite trick. Try it in your next match.

It sounds very simple, but Stanley Matthews was so good at it that the trick worked brilliantly nearly every time. And when it came to running, he was so fast the full-back never, ever caught up with him.

Two years after playing his first game for Stoke, Matthews was picked for England. In all, he played for his country 54 times.

Stanley Matthews was incredibly popular. In 1938 he had a disagreement with the Stoke manager and asked for a transfer to another club. What happened? Three thousand fans held a protest meeting, with another 1000 locked outside the packed hall. It worked. The problems were sorted out, and Matthews stayed at Stoke until 1947. Then – in spite of another protest meeting – he was transferred to Blackpool for £11,500.

A year later, and at the age of 33, Stanley Matthews was voted Footballer of the Year, and played at Wembley in his first F.A. Cup Final. In a great game, Blackpool were beaten 2-4 by Manchester United. Three years later, in 1951, Blackpool reached the final again – and again Stanley Matthews picked up a loser's medal as his team lost 0-2 to Newcastle.

Would he ever get a winner's medal? In 1953, he had a third chance as Blackpool got to the Cup Final once more, to face Bolton Wanderers. At the age of 38, everybody said this would be his last chance.

And, with just over 20 minutes to go, it looked as though that chance had gone. Blackpool were losing 1-3. Then, they pulled a goal back ... and Matthews started to weave his magic. With three minutes to go, Blackpool equalized from a free kick. Then, in the last minute, Stanley Matthews once again got the ball on the right wing.

What did he do? His favourite trick, of course! It worked as well as ever. Shooting past his full-back, Stanley raced to the by-line and pulled the ball back for his team-mate Bill Perry to whack into the goal. Blackpool 4, Bolton 3 – and Stanley Matthews had won his F.A. Cup winner's medal!

Frankly, I think Stan was faster before he became a knight!

For most players, that might have been enough. Not for Matthews. He was a fitness fanatic who always trained hard and looked after himself. He still felt great – so why should he give up? His record in the following years will probably never be equalled:

- He played on for England for another three years, winning his last cap in 1957 at the age of 42.
- Four years on from that, in 1961 and at the age of 46, he left Blackpool. To retire? Not likely! He went back to Second Division Stoke City, the club he'd first played for as a 17-year-old.
- In 1963, at the age of 48, Matthews won another medal as Stoke win promotion to the First Division. Their average crowd had rocketed since his arrival ... from 9,250 to over 25,000, and Stanley Matthews was voted Footballer of the Year for a second time.
- Two years later, the Stoke City team sheet still had his name on it. This time, there was a difference. It was able to say:

Right Wing: Sir Stanley Matthews

Yes, the Wizard of the Dribble had become the first

45

footballer to be knighted while he was still playing.

But, retirement was near. There was just time for one more record. On 6 February, 1965, Stanley Matthews played his last game for Stoke. He was 50 years and 5 days old.

So, now you know what it takes to be a top footballer, who do you want to play for? There are some pretty famous teams around to choose from. How about St. Domingo's Park? Dial Square? Or there's the biggest of the lot, Lancashire and Yorkshire Railway Company Newton Heath. Who, who and who? Read on!

Foul origins

The famous football clubs we know today started out in many different ways. For instance, the sound of church bells inspired quite a few teams to start up. Whether they called themselves foot-bellers and had teams with lots of wingers who played like angels isn't known!

- Everton began as St Domingo's F.C.
- Aston Villa was formed by members of the Villa Cross Wesleyan Chapel.
- Fulham started out as Fulham St. Andrews, after the name of their church.
- Swindon Town was formed by a keen football-playing vicar.

- Bolton Wanderers were originally Christ Church F.C.
- Celtic were formed by a priest, with the aim of raising money to feed the poor in East Glasgow.

Foul factory football

The other place in which men gathered in the mid-1880s was the factory in which they worked. As football grew in popularity, a number of these formed works football teams – some of which went on to become teams we know today.

Arsenal, for instance, was formed by workers at the Royal Arsenal Munitions Factory in Woolwich, London. (The workers made guns – which is why the club's nickname is "The Gunners".) They played their first games on a pitch behind the workshops under the name "Dial Square F.C."!

Can you pair these factories with the famous teams they produced?

1. George Salter Springs Works   a) Millwall
2. Singers Cycles   b) Stoke City
3. Thames Ironworks   c) Coventry City
4. Mortons Jam Factory   d) Manchester Utd
5. Staffordshire Railway   e) West Ham
6. Lancashire and Yorkshire Company Newton Heath   f) West Bromwich Albion

Answers:
1-f; 2-c; 3-e; 4-a; 5-b; 6-d

What shall we do in the winter?

Sometimes, a football club was only formed to provide something for a cricket team to do in the winter!

- Sheffield Wednesday were formed by the members of the Wednesday Cricket Club.
- Tottenham Hotspur (1882) were formed by the Hotspur Cricket Club.

48

The foul landlord's team!

Finally, one famous team started out as the result of a foul! St Domingo's Park, now known as Everton, played at a ground in Liverpool. This ground was owned by an Everton supporter named John Houlding. The club paid their landlord £100 a year (probably letting him watch games for free as well) and everybody was happy.

Then Houlding put the rent up – to a whacking great £250 per year.

The conversation after that was short and sharp:

And so, Everton moved to their present ground at Goodison Park. As for John Houlding, he'd suddenly got the next best thing to a chocolate teapot – a football ground without a football team. So he promptly formed his own team, and tried to call *them* Everton. This wasn't allowed, so he had to think again.

He came up with "Liverpool", and they've been playing at Houlding's ground – Anfield – ever since.

Don't foul me, sir!

Finally, some teams were formed by friends who'd enjoyed playing football (and kicking each other) at school and wanted to carry on playing the game (and kicking each other) after they'd left.

- Blackburn Rovers were formed by the former pupils of Blackburn Grammar School.
- Leicester City, then called Leicester Fosse, were started by the old boys of Wiggleston School. (It's not difficult to see why they chose the name Leicester – who'd want to play for a team called The Wigglers!)

There's even a famous team that was started by teachers!

- Sunderland were formed by the members of the Sunderland and District Teachers Association.

Who knows, maybe if you make up a team from your school friends today you'll end up beating Manchester United at Wembley!

Fair ladies football team names

The only trouble with team names nowadays is that they're pretty boring – all those Uniteds and Towns and Rovers. The names of ladies' teams are much more interesting. See if you can put together both halves of these names:

1. Villa	**a)** Roses
2. Doncaster	**b)** Lionesses
3. Millwall	**c)** Belles
4. Maidstone	**d)** Aztecs
5. City	**e)** Tigresses

Answers:
1-d; 2-c; 3-b; 4-e; 5-a;

50

Foul football kit

You've formed your team. Now, what are you going to wear? Some simple shirts, with just one colour – or something a bit snazzier with stripes or hoops? How about shorts and socks? Something matching the shirts, of course, with every player wearing the same. This didn't happen in the early days! It took some time for football kit as we know it to come about.

Your foul football kit timeline:

1872 Standard kit for a footballer was: "plus-four" trousers tucked into socks which stretch up to the knees, football jersey ... and bobble-hat! Every player in a team wore the same colour shirt, but they could choose whatever they liked for the rest!

1879 Footballer Lord Arthur Kinnaird could always be recognized on the pitch. He wore long white trousers and a blue-and-white cricket cap.

1879 A team called Sheffield Zulus played all their games dressed up as Zulu warriors!

1895 The British Ladies played a North vs South match. The *Manchester*

Guardian reported: "The ladies of the North wore red blouses with white yolks, full black knickerbockers fastened below the knee, black stockings, red beretta caps, brown leather boots and leg-pads." Not much different to Manchester United today!

1900 Racehorse owner Lord Rosebery persuaded Scotland to play against England in his racing colours – primrose and pink! The Scots are tickled pink as well ... they won 4-1.

1909 Until now, goalkeepers wore the same shirts as the rest of their team. Now they started to wear different coloured jerseys.

1910 Kit became uniform all over. The way a player could look different was by using a snazzy belt – elastic hadn't arrived yet, so he still needed one to hold his shorts up!

1911 Superstitious goalkeeper Dick Rose played his 23rd game for Wales wearing the same jersey.

He hadn't washed it since his first international in 1899, believing it would bring him bad luck.

1928 Arsenal and Chelsea wore numbered shirts – the first time they'd been used.

1933 Herbert Chapman (Tottenham) wore yellow football boots.

1933 As an experiment, numbered shirts were worn for the first time. In the F.A. Cup Final between Everton and Manchester City, Everton's players were numbered 1-11 and City's 12-22.

1937 The England team wore numbers on their shirts for the first time, and in 1939 shirt numbers were officially introduced.

1960 Football kit started to be made from a brand new light-weight material called nylon. Until now shirts were made of heavy cotton, shorts were long and baggy, and socks made out of wool.

1970 The first shirt sponsorship. England sign a deal with the "Admiral" company.

No. 7, great! My lucky number!

Lightweight!

Clubs aren't allowed to do the same though.

1972 Leeds Utd have numbers on tags hanging from their sock tops.

1980 Shirt sponsorship finally allowed. Liverpool were first. All their shirts now carried the name of the Japanese electronic company "Hitachi". Only one problem – they couldn't wear them when their games are on BBC TV, because the Beeb doesn't show adverts!

1982 The TV people change their mind. Now every shirt carries a sponsor's name.

1988 Replica strips started to be sold in the shops. Now you could play for your favourite team in the park!

1996 David Seaman played in goal for England wearing a red jersey with yellow, green and blue splodges, red shorts with yellow, green and blue markings, and yellow, red and green hooped socks. It makes the Zulus of 1879 look dull!

Foul shorts stories

Football shorts have seen many ups and downs over the years. Here are some of them!

Knaughty knickers

1904 The Football Association are worried about shorts coming up. A rule is introduced saying, "Footballer's knickers must cover the knee". It's not known what the ref had to do if they weren't – send them off? (The players, not the shorts!)

What a rip-off!

1921 Jim Bowie (Rangers) was playing against Partick Thistle in the Scottish F.A. Cup Final when his shorts got ripped. While he was off the field changing them, the player he was supposed to be marking scored the only goal of the game!

How many legs?

1960 Celtic become the first, and only, club to number their shorts instead of their shirts.

A bum rap!

1979 Full-back Sammy Nelson (Arsenal) was being barracked by the crowd after scoring an own goal. To show them just what he thought, he dropped his shorts. Arsenal suspended him for two weeks. More of a full-backside than a full-back!

Well, he has given a rock bottom performance.

Foul nicknames

York City lost that particular nickname when they sensibly changed their shirts

He's our new French player.

to something not quite so 'Y'-out! Then they returned to being known by the nickname they'd always had: "The Minstermen" (not Mr Men!), from the city's famous York minster church. Here are some foul football nicknames. Can you match them to their teams?

1. The Villans
2. The Pirates
3. The Rams
4. The Tigers
5. The Red Devils
6. The Hammers
7. The Foxes

a) Derby County
b) West Ham
c) Aston Villa
d) Manchester United
e) Bristol Rovers
f) Leicester City
g) Hull City

Answers:
1-c; 2-e; 3-a; 4-g; 5-d; 6-b; 7-f

Foul football grounds

Congratulations! You've been picked for your favourite team! Now, where are you playing? At a magnificent stadium, of course!

Can you imagine it? You pull on your kit in the warm changing rooms, trot up the players' tunnel – and hear the roar of the thousands of spectators who've come to watch the match. You play a fantastic game on the beautiful green pitch and then, when the game is over (or before the game is over if you've been sent off!), it's back to the changing rooms for a lovely hot bath.

Right? Well, nowadays perhaps. But it wasn't always the way. In the early years you'd have found things a bit different. Then there were some pretty foul football grounds...

Chronic changing rooms

- When Bradford City were formed in 1903, their players changed in a hut at one corner of the pitch! The visiting team were better off – they changed in a small room at a nearby hotel.
- Play against Grimsby Town, and you'd find yourself in one of the second-hand beach huts they used as changing rooms.
- And at Huddersfield, the players changed in an old tramcar – which was also used as a ticket office! As for lovely hot showers...
- When Arsenal first moved to Highbury in 1913, the ground wasn't finished. Players had to wash in bowls of cold water – and anybody unlucky enough to get injured was trundled from the pitch on a milk cart!

Pathetic pitches

The problem with many grounds was that they had previously been waste land. When football clubs took them over, they often only spent money on trying to make more room for spectators. The playing surface itself was often left exactly at it was – and that was often pretty foul!

- Blackburn's first pitch had a pond in the middle of it! For matches, this was boarded over and turfs placed on top.
- Northwich Victoria's ground had a stream running alongside it. This needed to be boarded over for matches as well, so that corners could be taken! Maybe this explains why the club were only members of the Football League from 1892-94 and then they sank out of sight!
- Port Vale's pitch was described in 1884 as having no grass on it at all.
- Newcastle's pitch at St James's Park sloped by nearly 6 metres from one goalmouth to the other.
- And as for Manchester United, in 1890 the football correspondent of the *Blackpool Gazette* reported that it was so often under water he'd heard that the club's officials had been taking lifeguard training!

- In 1884, a Scottish Cup tie between Arbroath and Rangers was replayed after Rangers protested that the Arbroath pitch was too short. It was, too – by 28 centimetres. Rangers, who'd lost the first game 3-4, won the replay 8-1.

Football grounds are nothing like as foul nowadays, of course. Or are they...

- In 1953 an F.A. Cup qualifying match between Runcorn and Witton was abandoned when Witton walked off after Runcorn had scored. Why? Because the ball hadn't gone between the posts. The Runcorn goal had a hole in the side netting and the ball had gone through that!
- The Reading pitch was covered in bald patches at the start of the 1985 season. Their groundsman had accidentally watered it – with weedkiller!

Did you know?
A traditional football match takes place every Christmas Day on Goodwin Sands, in Kent. Does one team manage to beach the other? Or are they always tide?

Foul weather
Football is a game played even in foul weather. And according to one newspaper reporter in 1900, over

Wolverhampton's ground, Molineux, it was very foul indeed...

> One side of the ground was lined with snowdrifts 6ft (1.8m) high. When four players, after an exciting mêlée, went into these mounds nothing was seen of them except for three boots! The match
>
> Page 15
>
> IT'S SNOW JOKE!

Sometimes, though, the weather can get just too bad to play at all. In 1947 the frozen winter caused the football season to be extended to June, and in the equally bad winter of 1963 virtually no football was played at all for the first six weeks of the year.

On another occasion, foul weather decided the league championship. In 1904, Everton were beating Arsenal 3-1 when fog came down and the game had to be abandoned. When the match was replayed, Everton lost 1-2 ... and ended the season losing the title to Newcastle by just one point.

Foul football question
How did foul weather cause West Ham and Millwall to begin a match in one century and finish in the next?

Answer:
Their first game, on 23 December 1899 was abandoned after 70 minutes because of fog. They were ordered to play the remaining 20 minutes when they met in the return fixture – on 28 April 1900!

Terrible tragedies

It's not possible to mention football grounds without remembering that, as well as brilliant football matches, they've also been the scenes of some terrible tragedies.

1902

IBROX PARK STADIUM DISASTER

The wooden terracing at Rangers' ground, Ibrox Park, collapses. Twenty-five fans were killed and hundreds injured.

1946

TRAGEDY AT BURNDEN PARK

Metal barriers snap at Bolton Wanderers' ground, Burnden Park. Thirty-three people were crushed to death.

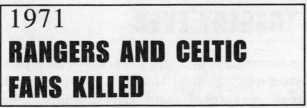

1971

RANGERS AND CELTIC FANS KILLED

Another tragedy at Ibrox, this time when barriers gave way on a staircase leading out of the ground. Sixty-six Ranger and Celtic fans died.

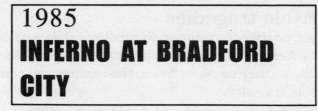

1985
INFERNO AT BRADFORD CITY

A fire rages through an old wooden stand during Bradford City's final home game of the season. Fifty supporters died.

1985
RIOTING AT HEYSEL STADIUM

The second tragedy of that awful year. Rioting at the Heysel Stadium in Belgium before the European Cup Final between Liverpool and Juventus led to a wall collapsing. Forty people were killed.

1988
WORST FOOTBALL TRAGEDY EVER

Europe's worst football ground tragedy took place at Hillsborough, before the F.A. Cup semi-final between Liverpool and Nottingham Forest. Overcrowding at the Liverpool end led to fans at the front being crushed against the fence surrounding the pitch. Ninety-four died.

Wonder-foul Wembley

If you're a footballer, the one ground you really want to get to is Wembley with its famous twin towers. All the biggest matches are played there, and have been since the Empire Stadium – its real name – was opened in 1923.

The ground took just a year to build, and cost – how much?

a) £750,000
b) £7,500,000

Building the ground was a pretty dirty job...

- 250,000 tons (that's 254 million kgs!) of clay had to be dug out to make the bowl of the stadium.

Then, in its place went:

- 25,000 tons (over 25 million kgs) of concrete
- 600 tons (610,000 kgs) of steel rods
- 1500 tons (1,524,000 kgs) of steel girders

And, to hold it all together:

- 500,000 rivets!

So, who owns Wembley Stadium? Is it:
a) the Football Association
b) a football club called Wembley
c) a company called Wembley

The answer is c) – and this company hires the ground to the F.A. for all its big matches, like the Cup Final and England's international matches.

This means that Wembley can be hired by anybody. Your school could hire it for a game if they wanted to – so try and persuade your teacher!

An amateur club called the Argonauts tried to get elected to the Football League in 1930. After failing in the previous two years, they applied again. This time they'd booked Wembley as their home ground! It didn't work. They still didn't get elected, and didn't bother to try again.

In its history, Wembley has been used by many sports. The track which the players run around on laps of honour wasn't put there for them – it's for greyhound racing. The stadium is regularly used for the Rugby League Cup Final, and it has been the setting for many massive pop concerts.

Did you know?

In 1968, Wembley was hired out to the organizers of a show-jumping event. By the end of the week, the famous turf had been almost completely turfed out! It took a couple of years to recover.

On this occasion, it was the horses who caused all the trouble. But on 28 April 1923, the day of the first-ever game at Wembley Stadium it was a horse who came to the rescue...

WEMBLEY CONSTABULARY
INCIDENT REPORT
Investigating Officer : George Scorey.
Supported by : Police Horse 'Billy'. (Distinguishing
marks — coloured white).
Report author : 'Billy'.

As my rider is still recovering from the events of
28th April 1923, this is my tale (Ha-ha!) — straight
from the horse's mouth as you might say!
    On the day in question we were summoned
to the Empire Stadium, Wembley. The first ever
F.A. Cup Final to be held there was due to take
place between Bolton Wanderers and West Ham
United. Arriving at the ground, I saw a large
number of people behaving like horses. That is,
they were jumping over fences!
    My rider told them to stop. 'Whoa!' he cried,
and I said 'neigh, neigh!' as well. It was no
use. This horse could have been an old nag all
afternoon and they wouldn't have taken any
notice. Into the ground they galloped, all 200,000
of them.
    What a nocturnal-lady-horse! (Sorry, I forgot
this report is for humans. I mean, what a
nightmare!). The ground was only built to
hold 125,000; where would the other 75,000 fit?
    We soon found out the answer to
that question. When we got inside there
were people all over the pitch, and none
of them were footballers. It was very
clear that unless we could produce a
stable situation there would be no match!
    I went to the centre of the pitch,
then started to walk around in
larger and larger circles. It made me
                                    P.T.O.

feel quite giddy-up, but it worked. Slowly I started to jockey people backwards. Finally, and although people were almost standing on the white lines marking the pitch, there was enough room for the match to begin. Our job was done.

Signed,

(Billy)

Don't ask me who won. We left before hoof-time!

Bolton beat West Ham 2-0, but it was the white horse known as Billy who became the real star of the first Cup Final. Unless you were the West Ham trainer, that is...

"It was that white horse thumping it's feet into the pitch that made it hopeless. Our wingers were all over the place, tripping up in great ruts and holes" — West Ham's trainer, Charlie Paynter.

"Spectators will have a fine view of the game from all points in the stadium" — match programme.

Ready? It's time for the season to begin! You're going to be playing loads of games against different teams from all over the country.

What for? Good question! It's time to look at the trophies you'll be trying to win.

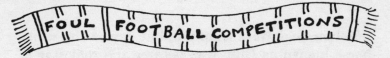
Nowadays there are pots of pots – usually called trophies – that football teams play for. But it wasn't always that way. Apart from playing other local sides in cup competitions most of the games played were friendlies against invited opponents. This didn't always work out...

Five foul excuses

Games were often cancelled at short notice, for all sorts of foul reasons. Which of these excuses were used?

1. The visitors arrived so late the crowd had gone home.
2. A star player wasn't available.
3. One of the teams didn't like the look of the pitch.
4. One of the teams had a more interesting game lined up.
5. It was raining.

If they think I'm going out in that, then they've got another thing coming!

Answer:
All of them – yes, even No. 5. To begin with, football was regarded as a 'fair-weather' game, and the teams would come off if it was raining!

The Football League

One man, William McGregor of Aston Villa, got in a foul temper because of all this messing about. His solution was to suggest to a number of other teams in the Midlands and the North that they should get together and play each other regularly in a league. That way, and by fixing dates for these matches, they'd know when and who they were playing for sure. What's more, so would the spectators!

In 1888, McGregor's idea came into being. The English Football League was formed, with just 12 teams.

Which of these teams were NOT in the 12?

ACCRINGTON ARSENAL BLACKBURN ROVERS ASTON VILLA BURNLEY EVERTON BOLTON WANDERERS STOKE CITY NEWCASTLE UNITED LIVERPOOL MAN UNITED TOTTENHAM HOTSPUR NOTTS COUNTY PRESTON NORTH END WEST BROMWICH ALBION DERBY COUNTY WOLVERHAMPTON WANDERERS

Answers:
Arsenal (joined in 1893), Liverpool (1893), Manchester United (1892), Newcastle United (1893), Tottenham Hotspur (1908)

McGregor's idea was a great success. The Football League began to develop its own rules, and to grow and grow...

League timeline

1888 The league begins. Points are: 2 for a win, 0 for a draw or defeat. After just ten weeks, the rule changes to give 1 point for a draw.

1889 The first league champions are Preston North End. They don't lose a match all season and are nicknamed "The Invincibles".

1890 The Scottish and Irish Leagues are formed. In its first season, the Scottish League sees 409 goals scored in 90 matches – and there isn't a single 0-0 draw!

1892 The English league is extended to 16 clubs and a second league division is formed with a further 12 clubs. Promotion and relegation are invented as well.

Foul football question
When did football teams play Test Matches?
Answer:
Between 1893 and 1898. To gain promotion, the Second Division sides not only had to finish in the top

---

three, they had to win a "test match" against one of the bottom three clubs as well otherwise the First Division team kept their place. After 1898, two-up and two-down promotion and relegation became automatic – until playoffs bounced back again almost 90 years later, in 1987!

1892 Accrington resign from the league. They're the only club from the original 12 who've dropped out.

1893 Northwich Victoria finish with a miserly nine points and leave the league just two seasons after joining it. They never returned.

1895 To decide positions of teams who finish with the same number of points, "goal average" is introduced. It stays until 1975.

Foul football maths question
Mudchester and Nutcastle finish in the top two with the same number of points. Mudchester scored 100 goals and let in 50, Nutcastle scored 50 and let in 24. Who wins the league on goal average?
Answer:
To work out a goal average, divide goals scored by goals let in. The team with the highest average is best. So Mudchester's average is exactly 2 which isn't as good as Nutcastle's average of 2 and a titchy bit. So, Nutcastle would have won the title, even

though they'd almost certainly been a far more boring side.

1898 Second Division Darwen's goal average is pathetic. They finish bottom, having let in 109 goals in 17 away games and been beaten 10-0 three times – one of them by Loughborough, who came second from bottom! Surprise, surprise, Darwen were kicked out.

1903 Arsenal join the Football League – the first team from the south of England to do so.

1919 Tottenham Hotspur are relegated – *5 years* after finishing bottom of Division 1! The league was suspended during World War I and they dropped down to the Second Division when it restarted.

1920 By now, both the First and Second Divisions have expanded to 22 clubs each. Southern League clubs form Division 3 (South).

1921 Division 3 (North) is formed, with 18 clubs. Southend finish bottom of Division 3 (South), scoring only 34 goals all season. Their top scorer is full-back Jimmy Evans, with 10 goals – all penalties!

1931 Arsenal are the first Southern club to win the League.

1938 Manchester City are the First Division's top scorers with 80 goals. Unfortunately, they'd let in 77 – so they ended up being relegated as well!

1950 Both of the Third Divisions expand to 24 clubs.

1958 Third and Fourth Divisions created. Clubs from the top halves of Division 3 (North) and Division 3 (South) go into Division 3, the rest into Division 4.

1960 Burnley become the First Division champions on the last day of the season – the only time during the season they have been in top spot.

1961 Northampton win the Fourth Division and are promoted...

Foul football question
How many times did Northampton Town get promoted or relegated in the years 1960 to 1970?
Answer:
Six! They started off in Division 4. In 1960/61 they were promoted to Division 3, in 1962/3 they went up to Division 2, and in 1964/5 they were promoted again to the First Division. Unfortunately, a year

later, at the end of the 1965/6 season they went straight back down to Division 2; were relegated to Division 3 in 1966/7 – and in 1968/9 were back where they started in Division 4 after being relegated once again!

1962 Accrington Stanley (not the same as 1892's Accrington) resign from the Football League.

Fantastic football names quiz

When Stanley disappeared, the league lost one of its most entertaining team names. Here are ten other good 'uns who have disappeared over the years. Which five were English and which five were Scottish?

1. Bootle (left in 1893), **2.** Lochgelly United (1926), **3.** Nithsdale Wanderers (1926), **4.** Nelson (1931), **5.** Glossop North End (1915), **6.** Stalybridge Celtic (1923), **7.** Vale of Leven (1926), **8.** Clackmanan (1926), **9.** Gainsborough Trinity (1912), **10.** Bathgate (1929)

Answers
English – 1, 4, 5, 6, 9; Scottish – 2, 3, 7, 8, 10.

1976 Goal difference replaces goal average as a way to encourage attacking teams.

1981 They still don't attack enough! A win is now worth three points.

1987 Play-offs are brought in to decide some promotion and relegation spots. Two years later, this was altered so relegation was automatic and play-offs were for promotion only.

1987 The bottom club in Division 4 can no longer beat the drop by applying to be re-elected. They're now automatically replaced by the champions of the GM Vauxhall Conference League.

1989 Arsenal go to Liverpool for the last game of the season. If they win 2-0, they're champs; if they don't, Liverpool are champs. Arsenal win 2-0 ... with their second goal coming from Michael Thomas in the last minute!

Foul football question
Which team signed Michael Thomas when he left Arsenal?
Answer: Liverpool!

1992 The F.A. Premiership is established. All the First Division clubs resign from the Football League and transfer to the Premiership, leaving just the Second, Third and Fourth Divisions. Since having a Second Division as the top league sounds a bit daft, the Second Division becomes the Football League's First Division, the Third the Second and the Fourth the Third – get it? In other words, almost every club is promoted. The only ones who aren't are the relegated teams – they stay where they are!

Foul football sponsorship question
The Premiership is known as the "Carling Premiership" because it's sponsored by the lager-makers, Carling – that is, they pay money to have their name splattered everywhere. The three divisions of the football league are now sponsored by the Nationwide Building Society, for the same reason. Who were the previous sponsors of the league?
Answers:
1983-6 Canon, the photocopier people; 1987 *Today* newspaper – who didn't last much longer than that, just one season; 1988-92 Barclays Bank.; 1993-96 Ensleigh Insurance (Divisions 1-3).

The F.A. Cup

Although clubs spend the majority of their time playing league games, the Football Association Cup – or F.A. Cup as it is known throughout the game – is an older competition.

It was started in 1871, seven years before the Football League. In all, fifteen clubs took part – one of them, Queens Park, from Scotland – and was won by a team called the Wanderers. When you see how they did it, you might think they should have been called the Wonderers!

- **Round 1** Their opponents, Harrow, dropped out before the game was played.
- **Round 2** They beat Clapham Rovers, 3-1.
- **Round 3** They draw 0-0 with Crystal Palace (not

the team we know today). There are no replays in the early rounds, so *both* teams go into the semi-final!

- **Semi-Final** They draw 0-0 with Queens Park, who then have to drop out because they can't afford the train fares to travel from Scotland to London for the replay. The Wanderers are in the Cup Final!
- **Final** Wanderers beat Royal Engineers 1-0, so with only their second victory in the competition, Wanderers become the first-ever holders of the F.A. Cup!

They went one better the year after, needing only one win to lift the F.A. Cup. How? Because, as holders, the rule then was that they went straight into the Final!

F.A. Cup timeline

1872

Jolly well played! Sorry, must dash

1872 Wanderers play Oxford University in the second F.A. Cup Final. The match kicks off at 11 a.m., so that everybody can get away in time to watch the much more important Oxford v Cambridge Boat Race!

1874 Queens Park, unsuccessful in the F.A. Cup, win the first Scottish F.A. Cup Final.

1879 Rangers draw 1-1 with Vale of Leven in the Scottish F.A. Cup Final, having had a

1885 Och no! My best suit! Mum'll kill me!

1887 26-Nil! We could have done with a bit less Hyde and a bit more Jeckyll!

1901 A flash in the pan. In a few years' time nobody will have heard of Tottenham Hotspur.

goal disallowed. Still miffed, they refuse to turn up for the replay and Vale of Leven are awarded the cup.

1885 Arbroath record the highest-ever cup score when they beat Bon Accord 36-0 in a Scottish F.A. Cup first round game. The Bon Accord side played in their working clothes, without football boots, and with a midfielder in goal. The bored Arbroath keeper didn't touch the ball once.

1887 Preston knock up the highest-ever F.A. Cup score, beating Hyde 26-0.

1901 Tottenham Hotspur become the only non-league side to win the F.A. Cup. They play in the Southern League.

1920 Shelbourne win the Irish Cup without having to play a final. The other semi-finalists are both disqualified – Glentoran for using a player they hadn't signed, and Belfast Celtic because

somebody in their crowd opened fire with a gun!

1921 Birmingham City have the shortest-ever F.A. Cup run. They forget to send in their entry form!

1927 Welsh club Cardiff City become the only club to take the F.A. Cup out of England.

1930 Arsenal meet Huddersfield in the Final – and the teams come out in pairs for the first time.

1946 Rochdale win their first F.A. Cup match since 1928, 18 years previously!

1950 Arsenal win the Cup without leaving London! They get four home draws, play their semi-final against Chelsea at Tottenham Hotspur's ground, and then go to Wembley for their 2-0 win in the Final against Liverpool.

1957 For the third season running, Leeds are drawn

against Cardiff. And, for the third season running, Cardiff beat them 2-1.

Foul football question

In 1960, Manchester City played Luton in a fourth round tie. City's striker, Denis Law, scored *seven* goals for City – and still ended up on the losing side! How?

Answer:

City were 6-2 ahead against Luton – all scored by Law – when the match was abandoned due to a waterlogged pitch. In the replay, City lost 1-3, with Law scoring that goal as well!

So, Dave, why are Wimbledon called The Crazy Gang?

1971 Ted McDougall scores 9 goals for Bournemouth in their 11-0 win against Margate.

1988 Dave Beasant of Wimbledon becomes the first goalkeeper to save a penalty in the F.A. Cup Final, as his team beats Liverpool 1-0.

1992 Liverpool v Sunderland. For the first time the losing team, Sunderland, go up to receive their medals first with Liverpool coming up

second to get the Cup. But get a bit mixed up – and Sunderland get the winner's medals! The two teams have to swap them later.

F.A. Cup fouls

You've won! And you're captain, so up you go to get the trophy. Or do you? What if it's too heavy, and you drop it? What if something foul has happened to it and you get up to the top of those steps to discover that it's not there...

Foul football trophy facts

1. The original F.A. Cup was bought for £20 and was 46cm high. Its nickname was "the little tin idol".
2. The cup was stolen from a shop window in 1896 and melted down to make fake silver coins.
3. A second, identical, cup was made. It was used until 1910, when it was presented to Lord Kinnaird to mark his 21 years as F.A. President.
4. The present F.A. Cup was made in 1911. It is 48cm high, weighs almost 5kg, and was made in Bradford. (Bradford City won it that year, the only year they've ever been further than the sixth round.)

The Football League Cup

Unlike the F.A. Cup, which can be entered by any club which is a member of the Football Association (and well over six hundred of them do enter it!) the League Cup can only be entered by the 92 members of the Premiership and the Football League.

It was started in 1960/61 and, in that season, not every member wanted to take part in it. Some thought there were already too many games being played.

Foul football odd-men-out

Five of these clubs didn't take part in the first League Cup; the other two met each other in the final. Which were they?

For the first six years, the final of the League Cup was played over two legs. Only in 1967 did it move to a single match final, taking place at Wembley.

Did you know?
The Football League Cup has undergone almost as many changes as Dr Who...

● In 1982, it became the first sponsored trophy. The sponsors were The Dairy Council, and the trophy became known as The Milk Cup! (Maybe it should have been called the Milk Bottle?).

- It kept this name until the end of the 1985/6 season. Then, from 1987/90 it was sponsored by the football pools company, Littlewoods, and became known as The Littlewoods Cup.
- From 1991/92 it changed again, becoming The Rumbelows Cup after the electronics company which sponsored it.
- Now, it's the Coca-Cola Cup.

Foul football question
Which competition was called The Mickey-Mouse Cup?
Answer:
That was the League Cup, too! It was the insulting name given to it by the clubs who didn't enter when the competition first started.

Four trophies you've never heard of
Competitions come and go. Here are some that have definitely gone!

The Amateur Cup

Nowadays footballers are footballers. This certainly wasn't always the case. When the F.A. formed, footballers were either amateur (they didn't get paid for playing) – or professional (they did!). Entry to the Amateur Cup was limited to the amateur teams. It disappeared in 1974.

Did you know?

Being an amateur didn't stop you getting a big head. In 1894 the Old Carthusians were so confident of beating Middlesborough and retaining the cup they'd won the year before that they didn't bother to take it with them. They lost – and the trophy had to be delivered to Middlesborough some time later!

The Coronation Cup

This was played for just once, in 1953, to celebrate the Coronation of Queen Elizabeth II. Eight teams took part, four from England – Arsenal, Manchester United, Tottenham Hotspur and Newcastle United – and four from Scotland – Celtic, Aberdeen, Hibernian and Rangers.

Who won? Celtic, beating Hibernian 2-0 in the final.

The Ford Sporting League

This was a trophy for footballers who weren't foul. Points were given for good behaviour, and for goals scored.

Who won it? Oldham Athletic ... and they've been the 'oldhers ever since! The competition lasted just one season, 1970/71.

The Watney Cup

This was a pre-season cup sponsored by the brewers Watneys and was played for by the two highest-scoring teams in each of the four divisions (excluding those who'd qualified for European competitions). Its first winners were Fourth Division team Colchester United, who beat First Division West Bromwich Albion 4-3 on penalties after drawing 4-4! The competition lasted four years, and was the first trophy ever to use the penalty shoot-out as a decider.

It's been a brilliant season! Your team's won every trophy going, and you've played like a genius!

Now what?

Well, how's your German? How about your French, then? What about your Croatian? Dear me, you'd better start brushing up on your foreign languages. Your team's qualified for Europe and you've been picked for your country!

We're off to play some foul foreign football!

Having invented the game, England believed themselves to be the only country, apart from Scotland, Wales and Ireland, who could play a decent game of football – and they weren't so sure about Scotland, Wales and Ireland.

For a long time, they were right...

International games

- **1870** A game takes place in London between Englishmen and Scotsmen, in London. It's hardly a real international because both sides are picked by the English F.A., many of the Scots being selected for no better reason than that they've got Scottish-sounding names!

Evans, eh! well, that's almost Scottish. You'd better play for them.

- **1872** sees the first *real* international between England and Scotland. In front of a crowd of 4,000 the two teams play out a 0-0 draw. Was it worth the effort?
- **1883** The Home International Championship begins. In this, the four "home" countries of England, (Northern) Ireland, Scotland and Wales play each other in a mini league competition.

Scotland are the first winners.

- **1886** International "caps" are introduced – and used! Remember, this was when players really did wear caps on the pitch.
- **1890** Cocky England play two of their Home Internationals on the same day, fielding two different teams. One beats Wales 3-1 in Cardiff, the other whacks Ireland 9-1 in Belfast.
- **1908** A team of England amateur players win the football gold medal at the Olympic Games in London.
- **1912** England retain the Olympic gold medal in Stockholm. It's the last time they get anywhere near it.

Foul football question
Where did an unofficial international between England and Germany take place in 1916?

Answer:
On a First World War battlefield. The East Surrey Regiment advanced on the Germans 'kicking footballs before them'.

And then it all started to go downhill...

- **1929** Almost 50 years after playing their first international, England taste defeat. They lose 4-3 away to Spain. The newspapers blame the heat, saying "beads of perspiration were dropping off the chins of our players as they ran about"!
- **1950** Disaster! In their first appearance in the World Cup competition, England lose 0-1 to the United States of America.

- **1953** The most famous pair of international thumpings in the history of the game. England lose 3-6 to Hungary at Wembley, their first home defeat at the hands of a team from outside the British Isles. Could things get any worse? Definitely. When they travelled to Budapest for the return game six months later, they lost 1-7.
- **1966** On top of the world again. England win the World Cup at Wembley.
- **1967** Scotland beat England 3-2 at Wembley, England's first defeat since winning the World Cup. The delerious Scottish fans take home bits of the turf as souvenirs.
- **1970** Disaster! Looking good in Mexico, England reach the quarter-finals of the World Cup and are 2-0 ahead against West Germany. Then the Germans score to make it 2-1 ... they score again to make it 2-2 ... and in extra time they score the winner.
- **1974** England, Wales and Ireland don't even qualify for the World Cup finals. Scotland do, but can't get past the first round.
- **1984** England and Scotland decide that Ireland and Wales aren't good enough, so they don't want to play the Home International championship any more. The result of the last ever competition? First Ireland, second Wales!

We think we should be beaten by a better class of team than you.

- **1990** England and Scotland stop playing each other. From now on, the Home countries are like foreigners. The only time they'll play each other is when they're drawn together in either the European Championships or the World Cup...

The World Cup

The World Cup competition had been going for twenty years before England decided to join in the fun. It had first been played for in 1930 and was organized by FIFA – the International Federation of Football Associations.

On the face of it, the decision was a good one. The early World Cups were quite foul affairs...

The World Cup timeline

1930 The tournament was played in Uruguay, and the host country reached the final, where they played their deadly enemy Argentina. Just to make sure that it wasn't too deadly, the teams were guarded by soldiers with fixed bayonets and, before the final itself, spectators were searched for guns!

1934 The finals were played in Italy, and again the host country were the winners. It wasn't plain sailing though. Their drawn game against

Spain was so dirty that 11 out of the 22 players weren't fit for the replay next day! **1938** In France, Italy retained their title. Again there was some foul stuff going on. When Brazil played Czechoslovakia, both sides ended up with nine players each. Two Brazilians and one Czech were sent off, and a Czech was carried off with a broken leg. It would have been 9-8 to Brazil, if the Czech goalkeeper hadn't played on with a broken arm!

Finally, England joined the rest of the world for the 1950 tournament in Brazil. The Home International championship was used as the decider and, as winners, England qualified. As runners-up, Scotland could have gone too but preferred to stay at home. England soon wished they'd done the same. In a catastrophic match, they lost 0-1 to the USA and failed to qualify from their group.

In 1954, in Switzerland, they did a bit better and reached the quarter-finals before losing to Uruguay.

1958 was a special year. Each of the four home countries qualified for the Finals in Sweden, with Wales and Ireland reaching the quarter-finals.

England were the only qualifiers for Chile in 1962, and got nowhere. Then came 1966...

The 1966 story

Everybody knows the story of the World Cup of 1966 – especially the Scots, the Irish and the Welsh who are always being told about it by the foul English!

After a dodgy start, England won through to the final at Wembley where they beat West Germany 4-2 after extra time. The match was full of drama. England game back from 0-1 down to go into a 2-1 lead with goals from Geoff Hurst and Martin Peters – only for Germany to equalize with almost the last kick of normal time.

Then, in extra time, England scored a disputed third goal. Hurst whacked the ball against the German crossbar and bounced down. The referee, after talking to his linesman, decided that it had crossed the line, and the goal counted. Then, in the final minute, Hurst ran through to score England's fourth goal, and become the first player ever to score a hat-trick in a World Cup final.

But you knew all that, didn't you? So here's some foul 1966 facts that maybe you don't know...

- Before the tournament started, the trophy itself was stolen from an exhibition in London. It was found in a front garden – by a dog named "Pickles."

- The match ball was stolen too! As scorer of a hat-trick, Geoff Hurst would have expected to keep it as a souvenir. Instead the German player Helmut Haller, who'd scored his country's first goal, stuffed it up his shirt and took it home to Germany

- Geoff Hurst wasn't picked for the first 3 of England's games. He came into the team for the quarter-final against Argentina, scored the only goal, and stayed in the side.
- That match was held up for 10 minutes. Argentina's captain, Antonia Rattin, was sent off for arguing with the referee and wouldn't go.
- When Bobby Moore, England's captain, went up to receive the World Cup from the Queen, he

realised his hands were muddy. So he wiped them on the velvet covering the shelf in front of her!

Since then, things have been fairly foul...

Year	England	N. Ireland	Scotland	Wales
1970	qtr-finals	out	out	out
1974	out	out	1st round	out
1978	out	out	1st round	out
1982	qtr-finals	qtr-finals	1st round	out
1986	qtr-finals	1st round	1st round	out
1990	semi-finals	out	1st round	out
1994	out	out	out	out

The 1998 finals are to be held in France. Will any of our teams get to play in the country of the I-foul Tower?

Foul foreign club competitions

For a club side nowadays, winning one of the major domestic competitions means much more than just that one victory. It means that the team qualifies to play in one of the big European competitions.

- The Premiership champions play in the European Champions Cup
- The F.A. Cup winners play in the European Cup-Winners Cup
- The three teams finishing highest in the Premiership qualify for the EUFA Cup

But it wasn't always as simple as this. When it was first suggested that British teams should enter European competitions, some people cried "foul"...

- **1955** Chelsea win the league and qualify for the European Champions Cup. The Football League advise them not to enter, saying they'll have too much trouble playing all the games. Chelsea withdraw, leaving Scottish League Hibernian to record the first British win in the competition, 4-0 against the German side Rot Weiss Essen.
- **1956** Manchester United are given the same advice by the Football League. They ignore it, enter, and beat Dutch side Anderlecht 10-0 in their first home game and go on to reach the semi-finals!

From then on, British clubs played every year in Europe. Their record has been a mixture of fantastic, awful – and a period when the rest of the countries cried "foul!"

Rangers were the first British side to reach a European final, losing to the Italian side Fiorenta in the 1961 Cup Winner's Cup. Two years later, Tottenham Hotspur went one better in the same competition and became the first British side to win a European trophy. In the European Cup, after a period when success just wouldn't come, first Celtic in 1967, then Manchester United in 1968 both won it.

This launched British clubs into a period of fantastic success. Between 1966 and 1984, the European Cup was won 9 times, the Cup Winner's Cup five times, and the EUFA Cup nine times.

British banned

Then came the Heysel Stadium tragedy. Rioting by Liverpool supporters before the 1985 European Cup Final led to 38 people being killed when a wall collapsed. As a result, British clubs were banned from all European competition until the start of the 1990-91 season.

Back with a bang!

The first season back it was again Manchester United who led the way, beating Barcelona in the 1991 Cup Winner's Cup final. Arsenal repeated the trick in 1994, but in 1995 and 1996 British clubs drew a blank.

It's a well-known fact that a footballer's career doesn't last very long. Most players have reached the end by the time they're 35. (This probably seems *ancient* to you, but it's not really. In most other jobs you can keep going until you're 65.)

So, it's time to think ahead. What are you going to do when you finish playing? Go and get another job, or stay in football somehow?

Many foul footballers do just that. How? By becoming foul managers, that's how! Read on for the lowdown on just how foul some of them have been!

96

Managers have a tough job. Think of all the things they've got to do – organize the players and decide what tactics to use, make the players believe they're absolutely brilliant even when they're totally useless, decide how much they're worth paying and try to give them less, decide how much they should be sold for and try to fool another manager into paying

more – making sure they don't fool you in the same way when you buy one of their players. It's a foul job all right...

Managers who didn't manage for long:

- Bill Lambton was manager of Scunthorpe United in 1959. He lasted 3 days – the shortest managerial reign on record.
- In 1968, Tommy Docherty managed three clubs in six weeks: November – resigns as Rotherham manager; for 29 days, manager of Queens Park Rangers before resigning; December – manager of Aston Villa.

- Brian Clough lasted 44 days at Leeds United.

Managers who found they couldn't manage:

- Alex Mackie was manager of Sunderland, then of Middlesborough. At both clubs he was found guilty of making illegal payments to players and suspended. He gave it all up and went off to run a pub.
- Syd King was West Ham's first manager, from 1901-1932. He did well, taking the club to the first F.A. Cup Final in 1923. But when the team was relegated in 1931 he started drinking. He was sacked after being rude to the directors and committed suicide a month later.

Foul formations

You're in the job. Now, how are your team going to play? In the early days of football, that wouldn't have been a problem. This would have been your line-up:

Yes, English football in 1880 was played with three defenders and seven attackers! When a forward got the ball he didn't pass it, but just dribbled with it until he lost it. (A bit like games in the playground). Great fun if you were the one with the ball, but pretty boring if you weren't! It was the Scottish teams who played football as a passing game. The English only started playing that way when the Scots came along and wiped the floor with them!

Gradually, though, formations changed. The forwards became fewer and the defenders greater, until this "classic" 1-2-3-5 formation developed, lasting up until the early 1960s:

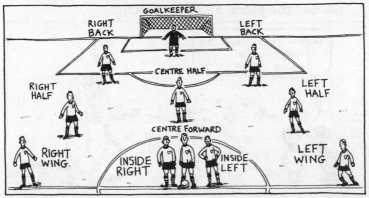

Formations since then have become bewilderingly different. Brazil led the world into 1-4-2-4 formations when they won the World Cup in 1962.

Then England played a 1-4-3-3 formation when they won the World Cup in 1966. Why? Because the manager, Alf Ramsey, decided he didn't have any decent wingers and told his full-backs to play there as well as in their own positions.

That's what managers have to do – make it up as they go along!

Fair tactics – or foul?

Managers have to come up with tactics to suit their team, and the match they're playing. Sometimes the tactics are fair – and sometimes they're foul!

Try this quiz to find out who did what!

1. Bob Paisley (Liverpool, 1974-83) would signal one of his players to go down after the next tackle. He'd then run on to the pitch to check how his player was. FAIR or FOUL?

2. Frank Buckley (Wolverhampton Wanderers, 1927-44) thought his team played better in heavy conditions – so before every home game, he flooded the pitch! FAIR or FOUL?

3. When Everton turned up to play Wolverhampton, expecting to play on a hard pitch and finding a swamp instead, Frank Buckley refused to let Everton into the boot room to put longer studs on their boots! FAIR or FOUL?

4. Instead of talking to his players before the start of extra time in the 1991 F.A. Cup Final against Tottenham Hotspur, Notts Forest manager Brian Clough chatted to a policeman instead.
FAIR or FOUL?

5. Frank Buckley again! Wanting Wolves to play with the right spirit against Manchester United on a bitterly cold day, he rubbed his players' legs with whisky! FAIR or FOUL?

Of course the dog's in on it. He's a RED setter.

6. Bob Paisley again. Once, when Liverpool were playing an F.A. Cup tie, a dog rushed on to the pitch. Paisley chased after it. FAIR or FOUL?

Foul training methods

Brian Clough was an interesting manager in many
ways. His players would run through anything for
him ... as they proved one day. Out on a training
run, Clough suddenly called for them to remove
their tracksuit bottoms, carry a partner on their
backs, and run through a clump of stinging nettles!

If anything, Clough was simply returning to the
old ways. In the early days of football, using a ball
in training was thought to be a foul way of doing
things. The players simply ran around and did
exercises to keep fit. The idea was that, by not
seeing a football all week, when Saturday came
around they'd want it all the time!

This didn't apply to Chelsea, though. In the 1960s
two of their players, Peter Osgood and Alan Hudson,
formed a "Monday Club" for training. Every Monday,
they refused to do any training at all!

Terry Venables had the idea of putting his players
under the influence. When he was manager of Crystal
Palace in 1979, he called in a hypnotist to work with
the players. At the end of the season, Palace were
promoted!

Malcolm Allison, Manchester City manager,
thought the players should hypnotise themselves.
He gave each player a photocopied sheet:

Allison lasted two years, from 1971-73. That's the problem with being a manager. Sooner or later, you won't.

More than anything, though, a manager has to give his team confidence that they can win. Nobody was better at this than Bill Shankley of Liverpool (1959–74). He'd turn up in the changing room and say to his team: "I've just seen the other lot come in, boys. They look like they've been out all night. They're frightened to death!"

Foul managers' rules

As manager, you can't stand any messing about. Your players have got to toe the line, not kick up trouble. So, what do you do? You lay down some club rules. Here's a rule quiz. Which of these have been club rules at some time?

103

Answers: All of them have been rules for one club or another! 1, 2 – most clubs; 3 – Manchester City; 4 – Bolton; 5 – Notts Forest (by Brian Clough on his defender, Kenny Burns, who he wanted to pass forward more!); 6 – Bury (a rule that caused a bit of a stink!); 7 - Middlesborough; 8 – Non-league side Peterlee Gamecock FC; 9 – Arsenal (In 1933! After Tommy Black, the Arsenal left-back, committed a bad foul in the F.A. Cup tie that Arsenal sensationally lost to Walsall, manager Herbert Chapman said: "What you did was disgraceful! you will never wear an Arsenal shirt again." He didn't); 10 – Leeds United. (As a way of encouraging team togetherness, manager Don Revie (1961-74) insisted on the players having a bath every Thursday – together! Hopefully he insisted on rule 6, too!

Foul transfers

One of the manager's jobs is to buy and sell his players. He tries to sell the useless ones for as much as he can – and buy players who are good (he hopes) as cheaply as he can.

That's got harder and harder over the years.

Your transfer spiral timeline.

1899 The Football Association suggest maximum transfer fee of … £10

1902 Alf Common, Sheffield Utd. to Sunderland £500

1905 Alf Common, Sunderland to Middlesborough £1,000

1908 F.A. imposes maximum transfer fee of … £350

1912 Danny O'Shea, West Ham to Blackburn £2,000

1922 Mick Gilhooley, Hull City to Sunderland £5,000

1925 David Jack, Bolton to Arsenal £10,000

1959 Albert Quixall, Sheffield Wednesday to Manchester Utd. £45,000

1961 Alan Ball, Blackpool to Everton £100,000

1974 Dennis Tueart, Sunderland to Manchester City £250,000

1977 Kevin Keegan, Liverpool to Hamburg (Germany) £500,000

1979 Trevor Francis, Birmingham

to Notts Forest £1,000,000
1980 Bryan Robson, West Bromwich to Manchester Utd. £1,500,000
1993 Alan Shearer, Southampton to Blackburn £3,250,000
1994 Chris Sutton, Norwich to Blackburn £5,000,000
1995 Andy Cole, Newcastle to Manchester Utd. £7,000,000
1995 Stan Collymore, Notts Forest to Liverpool £8,500,000
1996 Alan Shearer, Blackburn to Newcastle £15,000,000

Here are some foul transfer tales:

- In 1919, Leeds City were expelled from the league. Their whole team was auctioned! Individual players fetched between £250 and £1,250 with the whole lot fetching a grand total of about £10,000! One of the £250 players was Bill Kirton. He was sold to Aston Villa – and scored the winning goal in the Cup Final!

- In 1925, Arsenal wanted to buy star forward Charlie Buchan from Sunderland...

That was the deal. Buchan promptly scored exactly 20 goals that season, and Norris had to fork out the £4,000!

Foul tootball transfer question
In the 1932/33 season, James Oakes managed to play for both teams in the same match. How did he do it?
Answer:
He played for Port Vale v Charlton on 26 December 1932 when the game was abandoned. By the time the replay came around he'd been transferred to Charlton. Good decision – Charlton won!

- Jimmy Greaves should have been the first £100,000 player when Spurs bought him from AC Milan. Bill Nicholson, Spurs' manager, didn't want him to be stuck with that honour though, so he got the Italians to knock a pound off the fee!
- Between joining Queens Park Rangers in 1972 and leaving them in 1979, Stan Bowles made 34 transfer requests and they'd all been turned down. He'd just stopped bothering when he was sold!
- Clive Allen was transferred from Queens Park Rangers to Arsenal in the summer of 1980 for £1,200,000. Before the season started, and before he'd played a game for them, Arsenal sold him to Crystal Palace for the same amount! Was Allen bothered? Not really – his share of each fee was £50,000!
- It doesn't always work out like that. Before it became legal to pay players a signing-on fee,

different arrangements had to be made. When Jimmy O'Neill moved from Everton to Stoke, he had to move house as well. Stoke paid for a new cooker for his kitchen!

Moneybags!

Footballers earn plenty of money, don't they? Well, some of them do. Many of them don't. Money has always played its part in football, even when it wasn't supposed to. In the early days, every footballer was an amateur. In other words, they played the game for love, not money. Then organized competitions like the F.A. Cup came along. Teams wanted to win ... in order to win they needed the best players ... and the way to get the best players was to pay them!

This state of affairs – called professionalism – crept in slowly. In 1879, the little Lancashire side Darwen reached the last six of the F.A. Cup, holding the mighty Old Etonians to two drawn games before being beaten in the third. Their star players were two Scots, who'd been "persuaded" to join Darwen. Rumours grew that after each game pound notes would appear in their boots as if by magic. Were the rumours true? Nobody would admit it, but Darwen was an awfully long way to come from Scotland for a game of football...

Arguments raged on for a few years. In 1882, Preston North End were accused of using professionals in an F.A. Cup game. Much to everybody's amazement, Preston admitted it, saying, "Everybody else does, why not us?" Preston were thrown out of that season's F.A. Cup competition but within three years, the payment of players in England became legal.

In Scotland it took a little longer. Rangers, who regularly entered the F.A. Cup, found themselves drawn against a professional side. They withdrew in protest, and were fined 50p by the F.A.!

Two years later, Scottish clubs were banned by their own F.A. from entering the English cup. The problem then, however, was that all the best Scottish players were racing over the border to play for English teams! The move was on for Scottish players to become paid. In 1890 the Scottish League was formed. It was now only a matter of time before professionals were accepted in Scotland.

"You might as well try to stop the flow of the Niagara with a kitchen chair as endeavour to stop the tide of professionalism."

J.H. Macloughlin, who helped start the Scottish League.

In 1893, the Scottish F.A. gave in and professional players were accepted. So, how much did a professional footballer earn? When you find out you'll wonder what all the fuss was about...

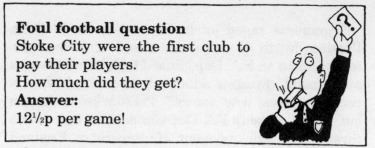

Foul football question
Stoke City were the first club to
pay their players.
How much did they get?
Answer:
12½p per game!

Sometimes it wasn't as much as that! In 1902, after the Stockport County players hadn't been paid for weeks, the players revolted against their management. Picking their own team, they grabbed all the gate money and shared it out for their wages!

Crikey! That's the fastest I've seen them move all season!

A footballer's pay was actually very foul for another 60 years. During that time, footballers couldn't be paid more than a maximum wage. For a while this was £8 per week, then £10, until by the 1950s it had risen to £20 per week. And you couldn't earn more than this amount however good you were, or whatever team you played for. An international player in a championship-winning side could be earning exactly the same amount as a player at the bottom of the Fourth Division.

Why was this the rule? Because it was thought that by having every club paying its players the same wages, there'd be less danger of just a few rich clubs grabbing all the best players. The players didn't see it that way, though. In 1961, led by Jimmy Hill the Chairman of the Professional Footballer's Association (yes, the same Jimmy Hill you see on TV) they threatened to go on strike!

Almost at once the Football League agreed to scrap the maximum wage rule – and from then on, players could be paid as much as their clubs wanted.

Was that a good thing? For the players, yes! In 1966 Ginaluca Vialli moved from the Italian club Juventus to Chelsea. His transfer fee – nothing; his wages – £1,000,000 per year!

Foul frauds

Wherever there's money, there'll be those who want more. As football became more popular, so did betting based on the results of matches. "Odds" would be offered for predicting which team would win a match, or for predicting that it would be a draw, or even for saying what the exact score would be. So it was only a matter of time before some foul footballers got their heads (and feet) together and tried to "fix" matches.

- In 1915, big bets were taken that Manchester United would beat Liverpool 2-0 in their match at Easter – which they did! After an investigation, no less than eight players (four from each side) were found guilty of rigging the match and banned for 30 years. Apart from one, they were all allowed to play again after the end of the First World War in 1918.
- In 1965, ten foul footballers were found guilty of fixing matches and sent to prison. Two of them, Peter Swan and Tony Kay (Sheffield Wednesday, 1960s) had played for England.

Butterfingers Bailey

One surprise result which wasn't as suspicious as it seemed took place in 1908. After a superb run of goalkeeping in which he only conceded three goals in five games, A. Bailey (Leicester Fosse) suddenly let in 12 goals in one game! He was accused of taking a bribe, and then the real reason came out. He'd been to a wedding a few days before the match, got drunk, and hadn't recovered by the time he went in goal. He was probably seeing two balls and didn't know which one to save!

The game's over. There's only one job left to do – say a few words for the TV cameras and the newspaper reporters...

Foul football managers' quotes

Bill Shankly (Liverpool)

If Everton were playing at the bottom of my garden i'd draw the curtains.

Tommy Docherty (Man Utd.) on his captain, Ray Wilkins

He can't run, he can't tackle and can't head a ball. The only time he goes forward is to toss the coin

Brian Clough (Notts Forest) on West Ham's Trevor Brooking

He floats like a butterfly – and stings like one too.

So, do you fancy being a manager after all that? No? Well, there is another job in football. There are good things about it, and there are bad things.

The good side is that it's a job that gets you right into the centre of the action. You'll get plenty of excitement, and for much of the time the crowd will be roaring for *you*!

The bad side of the job is that you can be sure the crowd will be roaring some pretty foul things.

Yes, you could be the man in the middle. The referee...

Who'd be a referee?

Some would say that being a referee is the foulest job going. Has it always been that way?

Your foul referee's timeline.

1873 The referee had a cushy job. All the hard work was done by two umpires, one supplied by each of the two teams. Each umpire looked after one half of the pitch. The referee's job was to stand on the touchline and make a final decision if the two umpires couldn't agree. Oh yes, the umpires didn't have to make a decision either, not unless one team appealed – like in cricket!

Wake me up if something happens.

1878 He doesn't shout any more. Whistles are introduced.

1891 With disputes getting more and more common, the referee and umpires change places. The ref moves to the centre of the pitch and umpires, now called linesmen, move to the touchlines. Each linesman has to run up and down the whole length of the pitch.

1894 Players no longer have to appeal cricket-style. The referee is given complete control over the game, making decisions whenever he sees something wrong. This doesn't stop the players appealing, of course!

Foul refereeing question

In 1894, Sunderland beat Derby in the longest league game ever played, but they were not sure what the score was. How could this be?

Answer: The game began with a linesman in charge because the referee was late. When he finally turned up at half-time, with Sunderland 3-0 ahead, he used his new-found power and insisted on the whole game being played from the start. Sunderland scored another 8, meaning that they played for 135 minutes and either won 8-0 or 11-0!

Did you know?

- During a match, the referee runs about seven miles.
- Referees have to retire at the age of 47.

- The referee's pay for a Premiership match is £300 – an improvement on the early payments. When the Football League began in 1888, the referee's pay was $52\frac{1}{2}$p. It could have been worse – linesmen only got 25p!
- Every league referee has to undergo a regular fitness test...
- and an eyesight test!

Tell that to one ref...
- In a game between Everton and West Bromwich Albion, referee Keith Butcher gave a penalty to Everton when everybody in the ground knew it should have been a free-kick to West Bromwich. That's when he found out – he was colour-blind!

Foul play! Red card!

One of the more dramatic sights in a football match is that of the referee waving the red card. He's only been able to do this since 1974 of course, as before that they weren't in use. When a player was sent off then, the usual thing was for the referee to point to the player's tunnel, as long as he could remember where it was!

Foul footballers can be sent off for four foul reasons:

1. Violent conduct such as foul fighting

2. Serious foul play

3. Foul language

4. A second "yellow-card" offence, that is, one offence FOULowing another!

There have been some other reasons, though...

Foul decisions

- **The team that sent themselves off.**
  In 1891, Burnley were beating Blackburn 3-0 when one man from each side was sent off for fighting. Blackburn didn't like the decision and the whole team walked off in protest!
- **The referee sent off by a player.**
  In 1930, Sheffield were playing Glasgow in their annual inter-City game. In those days, referees wore jackets but on this occasion the referee, a Mr Thompson, left his off and started the match in his shirtsleeves. The trouble was, he was wearing a white shirt – and Sheffield's colours were white shirts and black shorts. After a couple of minutes the Sheffield skipper, Jimmy Seed, asked the ref to go off and change, saying, "I keep passing to you!"

- **The referee who sent himself off because of the player who wouldn't be sent off.**
  When William Cook (Oldham, 1915) refused to leave the pitch after being sent off in a match against Middlesborough, the referee sent himself off, and abandoned the game. Cook was suspended for one year for his crime, which wasn't

much of a hardship because all league games were cancelled for the next five years because of the First World War.

● **The referee who didn't send anybody off.**

The 1913 F.A. Cup Final was the occasion for a running battle between two players, Harry Hampton (Aston Villa) and Charlie Thompson (Sunderland). Even though the foul pair frequently came to blows, Mr Adams, the referee, didn't send either of them off. Afterwards, though, both players were suspended by the F.A. for what went on – and so was the referee, for being too soft!

Did you know?

Fulham player Paul Went was a fluent speaker of Italian. Playing in a cup match, he swore at the referee in Italian, and got booked!

The match was in the Anglo-Italian Cup, and the referee knew the rude word because he spoke Italian too!

Six foul records

- Alec Dick (Everton, 1888) was the first player to be cautioned in a Football League game, for swearing at another player. Apart from booking him, the referee ordered Dick to apologise to the player he'd sworn at!

- The fastest sending-off was that of Ambrose Brown (Wrexham, 1936) in a Third Division (North) match against Hull. He'd forgotten about peace and goodwill to all men – even though the game took place on Christmas Day!

- When he was sent off playing for Hartlepool in the League Cup in 1966, Ambrose Fogarty completed a foul treble – that of being sent off in the three major competitions. Before that he'd also been sent off in a league match (1956, for Hartlepool), and in the F.A. Cup (1958, for Sunderland).

- Willie Johnstone (Celtic) was sent off 15 times between 1969 and 1983.

- Kevin Moran (Manchester Utd., 1985) is the only player to have been sent off in an F.A. Cup Final. His team still managed to beat Everton 1-0 after extra time. Moran wasn't allowed to go up and collect his medal, he had it given to him later.

- Colchester scored a foul double in 1993. Playing against Hereford, their goalkeeper was sent off for a professional foul. On came their substitute keeper – only to be sent off for a professional foul as well! Surprise, surprise, Colchester lost 0-5.

Foul football question
In 1996, during the game between
Peppermill and the Gardeners
Arms of the Blackpool Sunday
Alliance League, the referee showed the red card.
How many players were left on the pitch afterwards?
Answer: All 22. The person sent off was one of
the two linesman – for clouting a player over the
head with his flag!

Referees get used to being shouted at from all
quarters. But there's one insult, decided the Scottish
F.A. in 1996, that simply cannot be tolerated...

A certain John Neilson, playing for a team called
Easthouses Lily in the East of Scotland league, was
sent off. What did Neilson then do? Shout at the
referee? Bop him on the nose?

No. While the match was going on, Neilson crept to
the referee's changing room, and cut his socks in half!

The Scottish F.A. banned him for two years.

Penalty, Ref!

The forward's on the move. Past one player he goes, then another. He's into the penalty area. A defender moves in to tackle – and down goes the forward!

"Penalty, Ref!"

Everybody's looking at you. What do you do? Shake your head and run off in the opposite direction, or blow your whistle and point to the penalty spot?

You point to the spot, and the roar from the crowd can be heard in the next town ... unless you've given a penalty against the home team, of course, then you're wishing *you* were in the next town. Ah well, it's all part of the fun of being a referee.

Here's a ref's guide to penalty pandemonium...

1891 The penalty law is brought in on 3 March. Three days later, the first-ever penalty is awarded at Airdrie, in a Scottish League game. It then has to be un-awarded when the referee remembers that the law isn't due to take effect until the following season!

1904 By now, refs are getting the hang of things. Four penalties are awarded in a match between St Mirren and Rangers – 3 to St Mirren and 1 to Rangers.

1913 The first-ever penalty is awarded in the F.A. Cup Final proper, to Aston Villa in their match against Sunderland. Villa's Charlie Wallace misses it! (But his team go on to win 1-0.)

1924 Crewe Alexandra play Bradford Park Avenue and four penalties are awarded in five minutes!

1945 The rules concerning penalties are quite clear: the goalkeeper mustn't move before the ball is kicked, neither must any other player enter the penalty area. In the Scottish League game between Kilmarnock and Partick Thistle, the referee obviously knew the rule off by heart. When Kilmarnock were awarded a penalty, he made them retake it seven times for various infringements. When, finally, a kick was taken that he was happy with, the Partick goalie saved it!

1980 The referees don't see things Liverpool's way. They went almost a year, and 53 matches, without getting one.

Penalty puzzler

The referee can't win. In an international match in 1996, Ecuador were awarded a penalty. This happened...

Matamba of Ecuador strides up...

... whacks the ball into the net...

but his boot comes off and flies into the net as well!

"Take it again," says the referee. This time...

Matamba of Ecuador strides up...

... but whacks the ball against the bar...

while his boot comes off again, this time hitting the post!

"No goal," says the referee.

Afterwards they check the rules – which fail to mention boots going into the goal, hitting the post or anything else. The ref was wrong, and the first goal should have been allowed.

The world's worst refereeing decision?

On 25 May 1964, Argentina played Peru in an Olympic Games qualifying tie. The match took place in Lima, the capital of Peru. Argentina were winning 1-0. Then, with just two minutes to go, Peru scored, only for the referee to disallow the goal.

This caused a riot to break out in the crowd. Police tried to stop it by using tear gas, but instead they started a panic. Three hundred and fifty spectators were killed and one thousand two hundred injured.

Afterwards the referee could only say, "Maybe it was a goal. Anyone can make a mistake."

So, maybe you don't fancy being a referee either. In that case, there's only one thing left ... be a football supporter!

Trace your ticket! Root around for your rosette! Slip on your shirt! Scour around for your scarf! Rattle your rattle!

We're off to the match!

FOUL FANS

There's nothing wrong with being a plain old spectator, y'know. After all, it's the football fans who pay the entrance fees which help to pay the players and everybody else. Even if it isn't very much...

Foul football question
How much did ladies have to pay to watch football matches in 1890?
Answer:
Nothing. They were let in free. The minimum charge for men was about 3p.

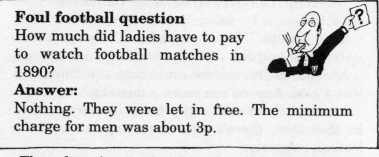

That doesn't sound a lot, but then you weren't getting a nice comfy seat in the grandstand either. For 3p, you ended up on a mound of earth behind the goal!

Yes, true football fans are prepared to put up with any conditions, however foul.

When non-league Yeovil played Sunderland in the fourth round of the F.A. Cup in 1949, they cashed in by adding stacks of extra seating. Fans who paid 37½p to get in, found themselves sitting on beer crates!

True fans

A true fan is one who supports his or her team come what may, through thick or thin, promotion or relegation, ups and downs, ins or outs, no matter what it costs.

Maybe...

- **The true fan watches the match.** In 1902, Gainsborough had already been relegated when they faced Blackpool in an end-of-season match. When a fire broke out in a nearby building, most of the fans left the game and went to watch the fire. The true fans who stayed to watch saw one of their team's only wins that season!

- **The true fan always turns up.** And sometimes they wish they hadn't bothered! In 1921, not only were Stockport already relegated but they weren't allowed to use their own ground for their final match either. The match, against Leicester, was played at Old Trafford. Just 13 true fans turned up to watch – and were rewarded with a 0-0 draw.

● **The true fan stays to the end of the game.**
With just five minutes of the 1979 F.A. Cup Final to go, thousands were leaving Wembley with Arsenal beating Manchester Utd. 2-0. They missed the most exciting finish in Cup history, with three goals being scored in three minutes as Manchester Utd. scored twice to draw level only for Arsenal to score again to win the match 3-2.

● **The true fan doesn't like being cheated.**
"Ticket touts" try to make money by selling match tickets at more than their face value. In 1959,

Third Division club Norwich City were having a brilliant run in the F.A. Cup and had been drawn at home to Tottenham Hotspur in the fifth round. When some true, but ticketless, fans met a tout who was selling tickets at over 15 times what he'd paid for them, they paid him face value for his tickets – then chucked him in the River Wensum!

- **The true fan likes to see his team win – but fairly**. In 1939, England were playing Italy, and the Italian Crown Prince was guest of honour. When Italy had a goal allowed, even though it was clearly handball, the Prince was so embarassed he wanted to go down to the pitch and tell the referee he'd got it wrong.

- **True fans chant for their favourite player.** In the 1970s, Coventry City used to have an advertisement which showed their team running out onto the pitch with the fans running out behind them. It had a caption saying, "This Saturday we're fielding 30,000 – make sure you're one of them." One of the true fans in this picture was a grandmother named Mrs Ridlington. Thereafter, whenever Coventry were playing badly, the crowd would start to shout, "Bring on Mrs Ridlington!"

- **True fans move about!** For the whole of the 1992 season, Arsenal kicked towards a North Bank packed with fans who didn't move and didn't make a sound! The ground was being rebuilt, and the fans weren't real – they'd been painted on a massive board behind the goal!

But what about when the football's at its worst, when your team is playing terribly, or the game is as boring as Maths on a Monday morning? Then, even the true fan can turn into a bit of a foul fan...

- In 1898, promotion from the Second to First Division was decided by "test matches" played out by the top two in the Second Division and the bottom two in the First Division. The problem was that they weren't played as knock-out games but as a mini-league competition. By the time Stoke and Burnley came to play their final game, both only needed a draw to be promoted. So, the two teams decided, a draw was what they would play for – and neither team even tried to score a goal. Finding they'd paid to watch the most boring game ever, the fans decided to make their own entertainment by pinching the ball whenever it was kicked into the crowd.

  Final score: shots during the match 0, footballs stolen 5!

Foul true football fan question
At the end of the 1966 Manchester United v Benfica European Cup quarter-final in Lisbon, Portugal, a Spanish fan leapt over the fence  surrounding the pitch. He raced towards Manchester United's George Best with a butcher's knife in his hand. Was he a true fan?

Answer:
Yes, he was. George Best was known as "El Beatle" in Spain because of his long hair. The fan just wanted to cut himself a lock of it as a souvenir!

Fans in action!

Most fans can only dream of playing in a big match. For some of them, though, dreams have come true...

True fans are there when they're kneeded

A fan played a big part in the first Scottish F.A. Cup Final, between Queens Park and Clydesdale, when Clydesdale's forward James Long smacked the ball past the Queens Park goalie and into the net. At least it would have been into the net if they'd been invented, but this happened in 1874, all of 16 years before goal nets were introduced. So what happened was that the

ball shot between the posts, hit a spectator on the knee, and bounced out again. The referee disallowed the goal and Queens Park ended up 2-0 winners.

Booting for Bootle

In the 1880s Bootle were briefly the top team in Liverpool – bigger than Everton, and certainly bigger than Liverpool who weren't founded until 1892! And yet, just before a match in 1881, Bootle suddenly found themselves with only eight players. Not so good when the match was an F.A. Cup first round tie against Blackburn Law! So Bootle did the only thing they could, and asked three spectators to play for them.

Honestly! They play in one match and they think they own the place!

Whoever the fans were, they must have been pretty good. Bootle won 2-1. Maybe they should have signed the fans on, too. When they played Turton in the next round with their full team, Bootle lost 0-4!

Collecting for Christmas

Brighton weren't so good at picking fans. On Christmas morning, 1940, they'd set out for a game against Norwich with only 5 players, hoping to collect a few more on the journey. (This sounds crazy, but it was fairly normal during the Second World War when players were stationed all over the country). Anyway, it didn't happen. By the time they reached Norwich they were still short, so they did a Bootle and recruited some soldiers from the crowd to make up their team ... and lost 0-18!

Foul football reporting

When real fans come home from the game, have
they had enough? Of course not! What they then
want to do is to read about the match in the
newspapers or watch it again on the television.

The media have been reporting on football ever
since the game began. And sometimes they've made
a pretty foul job of it...

Naughty newspapers

When the Football League began in 1888, there
were only two ways of finding out how your
favourite team had got on: go to the match, or buy a
newspaper. With no radio until 1927, and no regular
television highlights until around 1960, the
newspapers had no rivals.

At first, that was just as well. Before 1900, photographic techniques weren't good enough for good pictures to be taken of football action. Photographs of running players came out all blurred, not because they were too fast, but because the cameras were too slow. So, instead of photographs, newspaper readers were given real pictures ... drawn by artists!

With the arrival of better photography, together with newspapers like the *Daily Mirror* which showed plenty of photographs, the Sports Page arrived. And with them came the headlines...

Foul football report quiz
Fill in the gaps in these lines and headlines taken from the sports pages over the years!

1. **Although** _____ **63,102 people passed through the turnstiles...**
Athletic News, 1903

2. **Any one of our** _____ **teams could easily have given the Paris team of yesterday a beating.**
Daily Express, 1904

3. **The** _____ **sees Burnley win the Cup.**
Daily Mirror, 1914

4. **Our biggest international** _____ **for 46 years.**
Sporting Chronicle, 1928

5. _____ **, the Reds have won the Cup!**
Liverpool Football Echo, 1968

6. **Sorry, lads – you're** _____ **.** *The People*, 1971

7. **The Big** _____ **.** *Daily Mirror*, 1978

8. **Fantastic on** _____ **.** *Daily Star*, 1981

9. **Game, Set and Match to** _____ **.**
Sunday Express, 1988

10. **Ta Ta** _____ **.** *The Sun*, 1993

7. Snatch – after ITV had sneaked in and bought the rights to TV football from under the BBC's noses.

8. plastic – after Terry Venables had unveiled Queens Park Rangers' new all-weather pitch.

9. Wimbledon – after the Dons win the 1988 Cup Final.

10. Turnip – after Graham Taylor resigns as England manager. The newspaper had cruelly called him 'Turnip' Taylor.

Rotten radio

The first radio commentary took place in 1927. It was a game between Arsenal and Sheffield United. Thinking that listeners would be totally lost without being able to see the pitch, what did the BBC do – they gave them a picture, like this!

There were two commentators, and during the game they would both talk at once. The first would describe the match, while the second would call out the section of the pitch the ball was in. This was what an article in the *Manchester Guardian* said it sounded like:

Since then the radio has been broadcasting football matches non-stop. Look at any big match crowd. You'll often see spectators watching the match while they listen to another on their portable radios.

Once, a whole street did this...

Foul football question

In 1949, hundreds were locked out of the ground when non-league Yeovil played First Division Sunderland in the fourth round of the F.A. Cup. They listened to the radio commentary instead – even though portable radios hadn't been invented. How did they manage it?

Answer:

The police on crowd duty opened the doors of their patrol cars and turned their car radios up full blast so that everybody could hear!

Bite my tongue

Commentators often say some pretty daft things. Here are some from radio. Maybe radio commentators are dafter than TV commentators because they've been practising for longer...

- Tom Woodroofe, commentating during extra time of an incredibly boring 1938 F.A. Cup Final between Huddersfield and Preston, had just promised the listeners, "If they score now, I'll eat my hat" ... when Preston were awarded a penalty – and scored. It was the last kick of the game.
- Mick Lowes told his listeners, "And so it's West Ham 1, Everton 0, and that's the way it stayed through half-time..."
- Denis Law gave the listeners this gem: "There is no way Ryan Giggs is another George Best. He's another Ryan Giggs."

- And Simon Mayo showed perfect timing when he said excitedly, "And Lineker scored the equalizer thirteen minutes before the end. Talk about a last-minute goal!"

Terrible telly

Can you imagine it – no *Football Focus* on a Saturday lunch-time, no *Match of the Day* on Saturday night, no live televised Cup Final, no action replays, no Sky Sport, no...

Well, that's how it was until just about 60 years ago. Telly wasn't terrible – it wasn't even there!

Then, very slowly, the picture took shape...

1937 The first TV broadcast of a football match takes place. Viewers with a TV set (and there weren't many of them!) saw part of the F.A. Cup Final between Sunderland and Preston. They watch the most boring match in years.

1946 From now on, the F.A. Cup Final is shown live, and they're not quite as boring as 1937 either.

1955 The BBC begin showing highlights of mid-week games on a programme called *Sports Special*. TV football fans get some excitement, until...

1960   ITV televises the first-ever live game, a First Division match between Blackpool and Bolton Wanderers. It's a 0-0 bore-draw and ITV switch off again, cancelling their plans for further live games.

1964   *Match of the Day* begins in black-and-white, and on BBC2. It's so successful they switch it to BBC1, where it's stayed ever since...

Foul televised football question
Live televised football didn't begin until 1983. So how did television help over 104,000 watch the 1967 F.A. Cup fifth round tie between Everton and Liverpool as it happened?
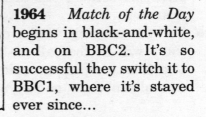
Answer:
By setting up TV screens in the ground. A crowd of 64,851 packed into Goodison Park to watch the match itself. Another 40,149 turned up at Liverpool's ground, Anfield, to watch it on huge TV screens.

Now, TV football reaches across the whole world. When the 1990 World Cup was played it was estimated that half the human race watched at least one game. Let's hope they picked the right one! Television football has had its hiccups, though...

Foul TV tales

- In 1983, ITV began showing live matches on a Sunday afternoon – and a man murdered his girlfriend because she turned it off while he was watching.
- For the opening weeks of the 1985/86 season there was no football on TV at all because the television companies could agree a fee with the football clubs. So, no pay, no play!

But for really foul football television, the only place to go is America...

Foul football on telly question
When, in 1967, football was launched in the USA, the referee kept on stopping the match when nobody had done anything wrong. Why?
Answer:
The games were being shown on TV. When it was time for the adverts, the referee got a signal and had to stop the match! This so confused the spectators, that things were later changed. When the ball went out of play or a free kick was awarded, the referee would wave a red flag to signal that it was a good time to show the adverts. He wouldn't restart the game until they were finished.

So, there it is. From broken bones to TV breaks, football has journeyed through the years to the game you play and watch today. The rules have changed. The kit has changed. What hasn't changed is the excitement and the fun of playing football. It's still the simplest, and the greatest, game in the world.

So, grab that ball!

Get out on the pitch!

Play football – and no fouling! (Well, not when the ref's watching, anyway.)